PENGUIN BOOKS

FAITH, SEX, MYSTERY

Richard Gilman is an eminent author, drama critic, and professor at the Yale School of Drama. A former president of PEN, he
has served as a literary editor and drama critic for *Commonweal*,
Newsweek, *New Republic*, and *The Nation*. His previous books
include *The Making of Modern Drama*, *Decadence*, and *The Confusion of Realms*. He lives in New York City.

A Memoir

PENGUIN BOOKS

FAITH, SEX, MYSTERY

by
Richard Gilman

PENGUIN BOOKS
Published by the Penguin Group
Viking Penguin Inc., 40 West 23rd Street,
New York, New York 10010, U.S.A.
Penguin Books Ltd, 27 Wrights Lane, London W8 5TZ, England
Penguin Books Australia Ltd, Ringwood,
Victoria, Australia
Penguin Books Canada Limited, 2801 John Street,
Markham, Ontario, Canada L3R 1B4
Penguin Books (N.Z.) Ltd, 182–190 Wairau Road,
Auckland 10, New Zealand

Penguin Books Ltd, Registered Offices: Harmondsworth,
Middlesex, England

First published in the United States of America by
Simon and Schuster, Inc., 1986
Published in Penguin Books 1988

LIBRARY OF CONGRESS CATALOGING IN PUBLICATION DATA
Gilman, Richard, 1925–
Faith, sex, mystery: a memoir/by Richard Gilman.
p. cm.
ISBN 0 14 01.0587 5
1. Gilman, Richard, 1925– . 2. Converts, Catholic—United
States—Biography. I. Title.
BX4705.G55114A3 1988
248.2'46'0924—dc19
[B] 87-20718
CIP

Printed in the United States of America by
R. R. Donnelley & Sons Company, Harrisonburg, Virginia
Set in Janson
Design by Irving Perkins Associates

For my daughters, Claire and Priscilla,
who will understand some of this book
now and the rest of it in time.

WHEN WRITING ABOUT ONESELF ONE SHOULD SHOW NO MERCY. YET WHY AT THE FIRST ATTEMPT TO DISCOVER ONE'S OWN TRUTH DOES ALL INNER STRENGTH SEEM TO MELT AWAY IN FLOODS OF SELF-PITY AND TENDERNESS AND RISING TEARS . . .?

—Georges Bernanos,
Diary of a Country Priest

FAITH,
SEX,
MYSTERY

INTRODUCTION TO THE PENGUIN EDITION

RECENTLY I SPENT AN AFTERNOON RE-READING THE MAIL I'D
received about *Faith, Sex, Mystery* since it was published last
year. I'd really had no idea what kind of response to expect;
indeed, like any author in his most self-effacing or, more likely,
paranoid moments, I'd considered the possibility that there
wouldn't be any response at all. As it turned out, there was one,
a broad and diverse reaction which ranged at one end from
denunciations of my account of religious conversion and withdrawal to, at the other, ardent expressions of gratitude and support. In between there were a number of letters advising me
that I'd taken the wrong path, that I should have joined this cult
or that sect, many of these communications being accompanied
by books and pamphlets proselytizing for the "right" way.

A few letters came from Jews who deplored my having gone
over to the "enemy," a few from atheists who deplored my having had any religion at all. There were a number from former
Catholics, who told me that my experience had been in many
respects similar to their own, and five or six from gay people,
who said that my having revealed a sexual proclivity different
from theirs but still "abnormal" was a source of comfort and
encouragement to them.

What surprised me most, I suppose, was that the bulk of my
mail came from active Catholics, who wrote to thank me for
having written the book. After all, this memoir contains some

rather harsh criticism of certain aspects of the Church, in particular its insensitivity—or so it seemed, and seems still, to me—to sexual dilemmas and the moral questions to which they give rise. Yet there were all those letters from practicing Catholics, laypeople, priests, monks and nuns. They were full of sympathy for my present condition of a vague faith without roots or a home; they assured me that I was strongly in their prayers and in a great many cases praised me for my "courage" in having written the book.

Well, I'm far from sure that I deserve to be called courageous. I didn't write the book as a "brave" act but as a necessary one, something on the order of catharsis or exorcism. I needed to come to terms with, and gain perspective over, my by now long distant past, so as to understand better the present through the exploration and recounting of the things I had done, or that had been done to me, during that time of quest, despair and hope.

The publication now of this Penguin edition of the memoir gives me the opportunity to say to both old and new readers that I've in fact gained some perspective, that writing the book did for me largely what I hoped it would. It hasn't brought me back to the Church, which in any case wasn't what I expected or intended it to do. It hasn't "justified" my life nor has it brought me peace—what could do that? But having written it has filled in for me a large incompletion, a hole in my consciousness and memory. That the book seems to have meant something to others, as a source of enlightenment or morale, is of course greatly satisfying to me.

The Penguin edition also gives me the chance to correct a few mistakes, most of them of minor importance, as well as a couple of typographical errors in the hardbound edition. More seriously, I unknowingly got wrong some facts about the background of my colleague at *Jubilee*, Jacques Lowe, and these are corrected in the present text.

Most seriously, I was in error about certain facts concerning

•

my experience with Etienne Gilson's book, *The Spirit of Medieval Philosophy*, and Thomas Merton's encounter with that book. Merton didn't take the book from the same library that I had, and his impulse to throw it out a window came to him on the Long Island Railroad, not a Lexington Avenue bus. Some basic similarities of a striking nature remain, but the connections between the two events were obviously less mysterious, less mystically engineered, than I made them out to be.

I can only explain what happened by saying that at the time, with my mind full of portents, with revelations of various kinds making themselves known to me, I was ripe for the creation of another "sign" from above. And so I unwittingly distorted the facts and kept them distorted in my memory through the years.

In no other respect would I want to change anything. To the limits of my ability I believe I was true to what happened, though, as several people have suggested, I could have written a much longer book. Yet as I said early in *Faith, Sex, Mystery* it isn't my autobiography but the account of one crucial phase in my life, a phase that, it seems, many other people have gone through. That my story should touch theirs in one way or another, that I should have been able to articulate some things on their behalf, is highly gratifying and, at the same time, a humbling confirmation of my belief that writers are agents, deputies of consciousness, not its owners.

FOREWORD

IF YOU BREAK DOWN THE WORD "AUTOBIOGRAPHY" YOU get "self," "life," "write." It sounds like a barked-out primitive command or the reply of an impossibly precocious two-year-old upon being asked what in the world he or she is doing with a pen and a diary. But of course the spiritual or intellectual injunction has always been "know thyself," not "write thyself." Are autobiographies intended then at least in part as instrumentalities of self-knowledge, means toward intimate discoveries? But most autobiographies, or their authors, seem to have all such knowledge already at hand, and anyway are more likely in our time to deal with external events and attitudes toward them than with mysteries or surprises of the self.

If you think about it, autobiography is a most peculiar genre or form. Leaving aside those done for quick commercial éclat, extended publicity releases concerning lives of only momentary interest, these books presuppose a particular kind of arrogance, a conviction that one's life is in some serious way exemplary, that to submit it to the scrutiny of others is a useful cultural act. Following on this an autobiography can be a means of at least provisional immortality, since it can imprint a life more quickly and thoroughly on public consciousnesses than can much writing behind which an author simply stands, the source and not the subject.

There's the suggestion of something godlike, the power to create oneself as though from scratch.

If you do write and publish your autobiography you remain from then on, to yourself and others, partly in the status of a literary character, a being created by language and infused with it; even if you want to, you can't ever afterward rid yourself of the gummy dimension of language, of literariness, with which you've coated yourself and which in turn attempts to model your nature into its own. You're stuck with self-appraisal in public and in words, a certain expressed stance; you're a self-portrait.

Whatever the motivation, it's a strange thing to do, this business of the self putting its own history into words: a life writing itself. And it's a grueling and precarious job, for obvious reasons: the mutability and trickiness of memory, the pressure of ego, considerations of discretion, and so on. It ought to be more terrifying than most of those who do it apparently think it is.

Isn't their provenance and embattled procedures the reason why autobiographies are always partly fictional (it goes without saying that fiction is always partly autobiographical)? I don't mean this in an invidious sense, as a warning to be skeptical, but simply that certain things have to be invented, made up: connections, replacements for eroded parts, maybe an assertion of purposiveness where there was really drift, or of understanding where there'd been bafflement; above all, what's needed is a shape. And certain matters have to be ignored or actively suppressed, and isn't this what fiction is implicated in when it chooses what it's going to be and not be?

When an autobiography or, more accurately in my case, a piece of writing of an autobiographical nature, a memoir, is undertaken from an impulse of only partial revelation, a desire to tell only or chiefly the things that *count* in the light of some idea or theme, then the difficulty is apparently narrowed but is actually stretched. This or that is irrelevant, you tell yourself, this or that is misleading or beside the point, if the subject isn't your whole life but what that life has been in relation to the governing idea, the subject of which you're a subject. Which in this instance is the awakening of my interest in religion, my movement toward conversion, the conversion itself, my deconversion (I think of a diver in a decompression chamber, to ward off the bends) and present existence in a realm of abstract, remembered spirituality.

How do I decide what is pertinent, what will serve and not betray the story of which I'm both author and protagonist? Is every moral or emotional crisis germane, every relationship I had, each bit of folly, each degradation or small triumph? Should I tell about my feelings when at fourteen I saw my presumably puritanical father stroking the legs of a woman who was supposed to be my parents' closest friend, or go into the fact that from the age of two I had a ragged scar on my nose, which later led some of my schoolmates to call me "Scarface," after Al Capone, filling me alternately with shame and odd pride? Do my eating habits matter, my taste in clothing, flowers, lamps?

We've learned, from Freud above all, that nothing in a life is truly irrelevant; we understand that history is alarmingly complex, the self's no less than the world's. And we've come to see that some of the decisive truths about ourselves have to be sought in lowly nuances, in backwaters of the mind, as a certain type of social history is now being fashioned from matter-of-fact, quotidian documents. And as if that weren't bad enough we've come to see how we're shaped by all that happened to us but never struck home, everything to which we were deaf and blind. Proust once remarked that the lines on our faces as we get older don't come from the ravages of experience but are the traces of all that presented itself to us but we turned down.

Well, I have to select, from among the obvious materials, naturally, and also, with effort and extended reach, from among the obscure, and I can only have faith that it will come out essentially true, which is to say that in the end I won't have written some other life, a revisionist history of my own, a paradigmatic and compensatory curriculum vitae. There are bound to be important omissions and distortions whatever I do (I can imagine myself chasing after the book once it's been published, wanting to insert newly recovered and clarifying memories in every copy) and perhaps some real, if not vicious, lies. But these ought to be overcome by the reader's awareness that such things are inevitable in an autobiography, so that armed with his or her common sense and the internal evidence of the book he or she should be able to correct them, in principle—as what is likely to have been true—if not in fact.

Besides, what I write about my life has its chief potential value in the way it bears upon the idea of religion and the actuality of spiritual experience as they took their course within me, a representative if I'm anything in the matter. This omnipresence of the spiritual idea and its fate, my sense of it as sometimes having lodged in me with beautiful clarity and pertinence and sometimes having merely fanned me with a distant wing, has led me to allow a certain number of meditative passages to insert themselves within the narrative, and to yield to digressions on a few occasions. In a book such as this the notion of relevance becomes problematic and that of appropriate form is under question.

And so I start, picking out memories, sifting and sorting, trying to reconstruct past time and vanished states of mind and to construct, on the slippery site of language and with its recalcitrant tools, at least the shape of what happened, its difference from what didn't.

Chapter 1

IN THE DREAM I SIT HUNCHED OVER A HUGE OLD-fashioned typewriter and stare at what I've just written. It's as though I've been transcribing from dictation and the words are in enormous uppercase letters, a single line, the well-known plea of Saint Augustine's: "God, send me chastity . . . but not yet." In my sleep it hadn't seemed funny, the way I remembered it when I woke up. But I didn't smile even then, for there was something in the air that went beyond the rueful witticism, some sort of disturbing reminder.

I hadn't for a long time had the impulse to address God, on my own behalf or anyone else's, and "chastity" wasn't a word I'd ever much used. But now the words, or rather the action they involved, prayer to put it bluntly, hovered in the air in front of my eyes, having traveled down the "royal road" which Freud said led through dreams to the unconscious.

I think of the dream again and see only the desk with the gigantic typewriter and a gooseneck lamp; the rest of the room is wholly in darkness. (When I was in psychoanalysis I used to keep a pad and a pen on my bedside table, to capture dreams in shorthand: Man . . . huge mustache . . . reminds me Tony . . . can't lift arm . . . garden hose . . . Switzerland.) And then it seems to me that a presence had been there, that the hound of heaven had taken up a position somewhere in the room. He hadn't been menacing though—he'd probably put on some disguise, or been defanged. Maybe he'd been crouched under the desk watching my feet for signs of impending flight. But from what? To where?

A few days later I begin to think about writing this book. I began it three or four years after I had the dream.

"I can't understand why you haven't written about it before," a friend whom I've just told about my intention of doing it now says. What she's referring to is the story of my religious conversion, an event that took place more than thirty years ago and then, after four or five years, was seemingly undone. Still, its consequences, or perhaps the better term is aftereffects, have remained within me all the time since, growing steadily more silent and invisible, yet with a small knot of indestructibility that doesn't show any sign of dissolving.

I look at my friend across a restaurant table with wineglasses, a green bottle in a wicker basket and an overflowing ashtray, all the butts mine. Her attitude, as nearly as I can make it out, seems to be approving, yet I don't think it's of the things I've told her but rather of the fact that I've said them, that I've added a major piece of information to our small stock of shared knowledge of one another. (Our relationship isn't romantic but that of informal colleagues, literary and intellectual companions.)

But a moment earlier I'd thought I detected a slight mark of distaste around the corners of her mouth, which I interpret as being due to her having had to listen to such an archaic tale, or rather a tale about such an archaic act. For I know her as a thoroughgoing secularist or, worse from my point of view, a person who finds religious belief—even the thought of having religious belief—almost laughable or pitiable in this day and age. It makes her think of the "born-again" business, which she despises.

Still, she's my friend and knows me as a writer and, being one herself, knows that writers eventually set down in one form or other, directly or slyly, whatever's been important to them. And so, out of curiosity and affection, she's asked why I haven't written about this most significant part of my past.

I give her a few tentative answers, which I'll give the reader a little later on. But first the long-deferred story has to begin. After I finish that, if everything has gone right, it ought to move into a set of reflections and a meditation—no, those words are much too lofty and disinterested; an "impassioned inquiry," as I imagine some sympathetic future reviewer with a bent for clichés saying—into what I feel and think about God after having apparently abandoned Him, leaving Him, as one might say, to fend for Himself.

At the age of nearly thirty an erstwhile militantly atheistic Jew, a boy who had been brought up in a home where the letter of religion was observed if not always the full spirit, an intermittently kosher household, depending on whether his maternal grandparents were living there at particular times, grandparents who spoke Yiddish much more easily and more often than they did English and, particularly his grandmother, had gestures that included a wide sighing shrug in reaction to what fate dealt them and a frequent clapping (or klopping) of hand to forehead when destiny seemed especially bitter, and who engaged from time to time in a mysterious and unpleasant ritual connected to death called "sitting shivah"; the boy who had been sent on roller skates to Hebrew school three afternoons a week and had held the speed-reading record there for some years (or until it was broken by a laser-eyed boy whom, he was later told,

everyone hated because he was fat and sweated a lot and was
so smart); had been bar mitzvahed with as much panoply as
the Depression years would allow, the gifts including the
usual fountain pens and a most unusual biography of Admi-
ral Byrd, he of the South Pole; had eaten gefilte fish, which
he disliked, for the sake of the horseradish that went with it;
had been filled with nausea at the sight of his mother or
grandmother eviscerating a chicken, arm plunged to the
elbow into the pale yellow creature's bowels, and could not
eat that meat for years afterward; was familiar with, even
though he had an aversion to using, such words as "goyim"
and "shiksa" and even "Gentile"; had regarded as terrifying
apparitions the nuns he would occasionally see going in and
out of—*scuttling* in and out of—the Catholic church a few
blocks away from his home in the Flatbush section of
Brooklyn, a church from which an endless and similarly terrifying procession of coffins seemed to emerge; who had
been pleased that his parents had given him the name Richard and not Seymour or Irwin or Myron and felt slightly
ashamed of that; who had thought of the names "Christ" and
"Jesus" as suffused with death, verbal coffins; and who late
into his twenties had thought of himself as an exemplary
product of a rational age, keen on art but on science too,
especially humanistic science—this person had become a
Catholic, which everyone will surely agree is considerably
more problematic and consequential than becoming a fitness
buff or subscribing dreamily to some Eastern cult.

There I was, a couple of days before Christmas of 1953, in
the cathedral of Colorado Springs (the building was a big
nondescript pile for which the designation "cathedral"
meant that it was the seat of the diocese in that area), a six-
foot, hundred-and-fifty-pound infant being bent backward
by a priest over the baptismal font in lieu of being held in
some gigantic godparent's arms.

The warm, no doubt stale, water trickled from my forehead into my hair and some fell on my cheeks, where it mingled with my sudden and embarrassing tears. But the embarrassment came after the fact. At the time, stricken and amazed, I had no thought that there were others watching. I was aware only of the soft voice of the priest intoning "In nomine patris et filii et spiritus sancti" and of the light touch of his fingers tracing the sign of the cross on my brow.

I felt like a tourist who has abruptly and unaccountably been made a citizen of some distant and enigmatic country, more remote than Nepal, without having had time to do more than sketchily learn some of the language and the laws. I felt like I was on a kind of Ellis Island of the spirit and saw (or much later did) my forebears sorrowfully or reproachfully passing in the other direction.

Just before the ceremony the priest had asked me what baptismal name or names I wanted to take, what patron saints I wished to have. These are saints you ally yourself with at baptism—in the vast majority of cases of course they're assigned by parents—so that you're supposed to come under their wings and have special access to them. You can also choose the Virgin Mary or one of the angels like Gabriel, but you don't choose Christ; I wouldn't have called myself or thought of myself as Richard Jesus Gilman, though for some reason people from Spanish cultures have always liked to take that name.

But Richard Joan Thomas Gilman was permissible. I hadn't thought about it before that evening and had to decide quickly. But I knew at once whom I wanted: Joan of Arc and Thomas More. Two "secular" saints, one could say, two from the world and therefore not nearly as remote from me as the more usual kind, the ones that struck me as nothing but saints, nothing but Catholic. Thomas More, a writer and statesman and intellectual, a valorous lovely man; I had recently read a biography of him. And Joan, the "astounding virgin," as a contemporary chronicler had called her, yes Joan (a man can take a woman's name in this matter and vice versa) had along with Amelia Earhart been the Beatrice of my youth.

An hour or so later as I was driving back to the rooming house where I was staying, through the deserted snow-covered streets and the frosty air, I pulled to a stop in the middle of an intersection and burst into a flood of tears. They came from relief, fear of the unknown life that awaited me, the sense of having done something irrevocable that was at once alarming and potentially full of solace.

A prowl car pulled up and the cop got out, walked over to my car in the shambling yet wary way they do it, bent down, looked in at me and asked if there was any trouble. Through my tears I told him that I had just come from being baptized as a Catholic, wanting crazily to add, "I've just been made the property of God." Maybe I really did say that, because the policeman ran his tongue over his lips and studied me for a while. Then he asked me where I lived and told me to follow his own car to my place.

A little while before, in the moments after the ritual, we had been sitting in the dismal, puce-colored rectory and sipping glasses of bad wine. It was a small group: the youthful priest who had instructed and baptized me and who to my astonishment had revealed several weeks earlier that he too had been converted from Judaism (though I never learned the details) and a young couple, strangers to me before that night, who had been pressed into service to act technically as my godparents and whom I was never to see again after that night. I've sometimes wondered if they remembered my name and, if so, whether or not they ever read anything I've written.

During the strained conversation I'd been miles away and

had found myself thinking of a book I had read a year or so before, *The Tragic Sense of Life* by the Spanish novelist and philosopher Miguel de Unamuno. It was a feverish account of faith and in it he had said something that had struck me sharply, which was that whenever he met a person who didn't believe in a life after death he had no trouble understanding and accepting that, but what he couldn't understand or accept was that there were people who actually didn't *want* to believe in eternal life. Such a thing filled him with angry bafflement.

Though it was to have a profound effect on me, I recognized that there was something bullying about this remark of Unamuno, who had a marvelously vigorous and original mind, but who like all scary prophets was furiously impatient and intolerant. I think there's always something bullying about processes of conversion, about all kinds of moral or spiritual persuasion for that matter. A rough elbow nudges you in the direction of the True and the Good; you're jostled into a corner where a big hard confident belly cuts off your retreat; your questions are stopped with an upraised hand and the single word "later."

Still, I wasn't an innocent victim in this case; I'd lent myself to Unamuno's bullying by conniving in the aggression. For I, too, throughout all the years when I had been an unbeliever had always thought it strange, even perverse, not at least to want to live forever. I didn't call what I secretly longed for "eternal life"; I'm sure the phrase didn't mean anything to me when I was young. Nor did the word "immortality" mean anything to me, at any rate not until I'd gained some sort of culture, a literary sensibility, after which I could think about the question and use the word for the type of indestructibility or deathlessness it was possible to achieve through the creation of works of art or thought. Moreover, I had never had any physical conception of an afterlife, no scenario for it; I didn't even try to imagine what existence might be like after my physical life was over, although I remember scoffing at the *Green Pastures* type of arrangement.

There had been scarcely any theology in the teaching at the Hebrew school I'd gone to, where the curriculum could only be called "studies" by an act of generosity. What we went through there was almost entirely a matter of rote learning and the inculcation of pride in being Jewish (I remember our purple and yellow satin basketball uniforms had a Star of David on the shorts), and when later I did learn something about Jewish teaching on the subject of the afterlife I remember it as being extraordinarily vague and indecisive; it promised almost nothing.

So my desire was almost entirely secular, with nothing spiritual in it, except that it was my spirit, even more than my body, I hoped would survive. My hope had no eschatological dimension, nor did it have anything to do with moral judgment of any sort; there was nothing in it of Heaven and Hell, which were in fact words or ideas I thought mere superstitions. No, the thing I wanted was simply—simply!— not to be obliterated, not to have to come down to a day, a moment, when there would be nothing more I would be allowed to do or say or see or think.

In my late teens I had been a fervent admirer of the novels of Thomas Wolfe and I bring to mind now one of those plangent, callow phrases that run through his writing, mottoes of adolescent bravado: "For we were twenty and would never die." I half believed it or wanted to, but in reality, beneath the imperviousness of my youthful energy and the vein of optimism based on an incalculably long future, I always knew that I *would* die and I couldn't bear knowing it. That's what Unamuno meant, it seemed to me, beneath the anguished theology, the fierce Catholic—or at least as much Spanish thinking—which at the time I read his book I was in no position to understand or judge. What he meant and what in fact he several times literally said was: I don't want to be *obliterated*. (And now I stop writing to track down something vaguely remembered from William James's *The Varieties of Religious Experience:* "For the great majority of our own race [religion] *means* immortality and nothing else.")

I remember once getting into a raucous argument with my two closest boyhood friends over the question of whether there would be a life after death. We must have been about eleven or twelve and so it couldn't have been all that long since we'd begun to assimilate and deal with the notion of death itself. Yet there we were, standing on a street corner in Brooklyn on a freezing winter afternoon, bundled in our windbreakers, corduroy knickers, wool stockings and wool caps with tassels, engaged in a shouting match about what would happen after we were dead. My friends (oh, Bobby! oh, Sandy!), stickball and touch football and roller-hockey companions, the kids I went ritually to the movies with every Saturday afternoon, insisted, little realists, snotty juvenile rationalists that they were, that there wouldn't be anything more, that we'd simply die and that would be it. I guess it was the first time I'd heard anyone say something like "when you're dead, you're dead," and I winced at it.

For I, who had no inkling of what it might be like later, *afterward*, and no religious conviction or belief, only a raw or sullen hunger, had a suspicion that they were probably right. But I also felt an edge of contempt for them. There seemed to be something deficient in their attitude; I thought it mean and unworthy. I couldn't begin to formulate it at the time but it was as though I saw them already cast in some

mold of passive acceptance of fate, held by a tight propriety
in the face of mystery, a condition they'd be in to the end. I
thought, without using a word I didn't know at the time,
that they were bourgeois. And from then on, in a way I
hadn't before but was to do through all the years I stayed
spiritually unsatisfied, I thought of myself, without much
satisfaction, as "different."

At any rate Unamuno, who seemed to have information
on how immortality might be obtained, and who conferred a
sort of legitimacy on my own craving for it, even though
when I read his book I had pushed aside all the specifically
Catholic arguments in it, was a factor leading up to my conversion, especially after I'd become able to understand the
theology of his passion. But sitting uncomfortably in that
rectory, as alien a place as I'd ever been in, with its heavy
dark wooden furniture, its kitschy crucifix on the wall and
its stagnant odors, I thought of him not as a force directly
behind what had just happened to me but as a kind of men-
tor or friend. It was as though I were saying to him, all right,
listen to me, I'm not one of those people who disgust you
with their lack of imagination, their indomitable levelhead-
edness, I'm one of your boys now. I've gone and done it. I've
acted to protect myself from erasure and I hope to hell
you're right about this being the way.

So Unamuno was indeed a powerful confirming voice in
my ear, as other writers were, but he surely wasn't the *reason* I'd become a Catholic. You don't take such an unimaginable step as this one was for me as a result of someone's
argument or testimony or even as the clear outcome of a long
process of intellectual cause and effect. In my case the whole
affair was from the beginning a great jumble of hungers,
fears, beliefs and counterbeliefs, persuasions and influences,
leaps and retreats, false starts, alternating states of paralysis

and energy. Or I could describe it as a series of propulsions of different kinds and intensities in which I had suddenly been caught up and against which, all the time I was being kicked and shoved and cajoled and tugged and seduced and hauled along, I fought doggedly, sometimes with my eyes open and sometimes not.

Social scientists, and journalists more crudely, are forever trying to find out the "reasons" why people do what they do, investigations that become truly absurd when the acts are extreme or atrocious and so may be said to encompass the whole self. One day I heard on my car radio a newscaster tell about a man who that morning had killed his wife, their four children and himself. "The police have not yet determined the motive," the newsman finished by saying. I gasped at the inanity of the remark.

How can so calamitous and mysteriously absolute an act have a single, unambiguous motive? The man committed murder and suicide, wiped out everything because of *everything*, because his whole life came down in horror and despair to that unimaginable moment. The horror and despair may not have been in his consciousness; perhaps he did it all mechanically, in a stupor of destruction. But they were in him nevertheless. I remember Charles Péguy's remark that we don't die from our deaths but from our entire lives. I came to my conversion, which, without wanting to be dramatic about it, I can describe as a kind of death, the end of a previous life, out of everything that had gone on in me, all that had happened to me before.

I've said that I can never escape my conversion, even though by now it almost seems as though it was done by, or happened to, someone else. But it isn't that I haven't wanted to get rid of it or haven't tried. Far from it. I haven't practiced Catholicism—been to Mass, gone to Confession, presented my forehead for a smudge on Ash Wednesday—for more than twenty years. I've certainly succeeded in exiling the whole thing to some remote place in my consciousness. But shove something like that into the furthest recesses of your soul and memory, and it's still there. And how painful it is to get in touch with it again. No, not so much painful as wildly disorienting; in which direction am I facing? I thought that view had been cut off.

When Rimbaud was dying of gangrene in a Marseilles hospital after he'd left his degrading life as a gunrunner and slave trader in Abyssinia and gone back to France, his sister came to stay at his bedside. A day or two before he died, she tells us, he asked her to send for a priest, and she, much amazed and distressed, said to him in some such words as these: "But, Arthur, you've been so far away from all that, your life has been so . . . I just don't understand." To which, she says, he replied, "I am a victim of my own baptism."

As presumptuous as it might seem to identify in this way with Rimbaud, I feel much the same way. And I suspect that many Catholics (and doubtless some Protestants too) but especially converts, who are accomplices in the act of their baptism in a way infants can't possibly be, and including those who like me have "fallen away" as far as it seems possible to go—that such people somewhere and in some manner feel like "victims" in Rimbaud's sense.

In this regard one of the things I want to talk about is the condition of *having been* religious, what it's like to have lived once in a double way, in two kinds of time, as it were, within two spaces, and then to return to the single mode of a life which whatever else it may be is one without transcendence. What remains? What has been lost? Is there nostalgia for the certainties (but I was never really certain), for clear moral judgments (but they were never wholly clear to me)?

And what of regret, remorse, the thin edge of a sense of betrayal?

To go back to the question my friend asked about my having waited so long before writing about my conversion. Well, to begin with, the conversion story is an instigation to something larger, or at least less easily defined and circumscribed, which is the question of religion in relation to other things, art, sex, moral life, intellectual being, in all of which confrontations I was once caught.

But why did I wait? It may have been due to genuine modesty (unlikely) or fear, or a kind of exquisitely subtle pride, and it may be that I'll find out only after I've finished the book. Alain Robbe-Grillet once said that a writer writes a particular book in order to find out why he or she wanted to write it, and I think that's partly the case with me now. Yet I can say something about what I was thinking along these lines after the event took place and during all those years I kept putting the writing off.

To begin with, there's this question: who was I at the time to tell such a story? I'd done nothing in the world that anyone had taken notice of and little that they hadn't. All that distinguished me was that this conversion had happened to me, which is more accurate than to say I chose it. And so I thought that unless you're a terrific writer, a genius, a story like this gets its justification and cachet from *who* you are, and I was nobody. Then, some years later when I'd begun to make some headway in a career and gained some small reputation, I saw the conversion as having passed from a wholly private event to a potentially public fact about me and I feared that I would now become classifiable by others and therefore subject to a particularly obnoxious process of reduction, the maniacal categorization by which everyone in our society is inserted into one or another typology.

Something far more significant was this: about five years after my baptism I began to find myself less and less able to practice the Faith, more and more restless and unhappy with it. It dwindled and seemed to expire in me, though it remained for a time as a disposition or desire and Rimbaud's type of spear still had its point stuck in me, as it continues almost imperceptibly to do.

When my faith started to erode it seemed to me that even such authority as I might earlier have possessed, one based not on reputation or accomplishment, it went without saying, but on a position as naive witness, was now gone. And then, unconvinced by all these explanations, I found myself becoming ashamed of *not having spoken* before, with the result that the recognition of my cowardice left me more speechless still, as such a thing has a way of doing. I mean I was silent in public; those closest to me always knew about my Catholicism, along with an occasional new friend or even a stranger to whom I saw some point in communicating it.

This may all be rationalization, but I expect to find that out. Anyway, if I think the time is beckoning now to write about my religious conversion and about religion more broadly, it's not out of a grand change of heart or a newly acquired insouciance but out of a sense of the confluence between my own history and present state of being and the new circumstances of consciousness around me. By this I mean that the ideal, hypothetical reader whom Paul Valéry once said every writer first invents and then tries to find in actuality may now be present in my mind and at the same time be out there in perhaps modest numbers.

That's how I discovered him or her out there: by extension. I've come to think that I can't be the only person in this exceedingly secular society, secular at its core despite the fundamentalist twitchings on the surface, who suspects that it may be the right time to consider another possibility, or at least throw a glance at it. I don't mean that we ought to be looking for a way out, an "answer" to the ills of the time. There isn't going to be any evangelism in these pages or any prescriptions.

I just want to prowl around the idea of the spiritual, acknowledging that it's there, or was once there for me, poor, ruined, discredited and ill-equipped to present itself as it is, and to listen to its strange voice, if indeed it has one, muted or harsh. My own story might then be an exemplification of such a spiritual possibility, the report of a journey to the frontier, a sojourn there and a retreat. Or it might be a cautionary tale, depending on one's point of view.

The unfashionableness of the spiritual and of religion in general in the "brighter," more enlightened sectors of society, the ones I professionally belong to, the odd, almost offensive quality of its whole vocabulary—faith, transcendence, soul, eternal life, God—all this seems to me precisely a solicitation to take it up again. For whatever is fashionable or unfashionable in such realms as these is by that token suspect. Certainly the born-again movement is deeply suspect, and implacable irreligion may be too. For fashion is a form of tyranny as well as a sign of boredom, and unfashionableness may be a sign of disappointment. It may seem frivolous to talk about religion in such terms—was it "fashionable" to be religious in the Middle Ages?—but my point is that we're carried along in matters of the psyche and the spirit by our place and time, we're held more or less firmly in tow, so that to examine whatever is excluded on principle by the age, or some part of it, may be idle or foolish but is surely some sort of act of freedom. At least I've told myself that, and I feel now in my unbelief oddly moved by a sense of pity for religion's fragility, the defeatedness of what it represents to so many people in these days.

The soul, the spirit. "Where, what, is it?" Robert Musil

wrote in *The Man Without Qualities.* "Perhaps," he went on, "if we knew more about it, there would be an awkward silence around this noun 'spirit.'" If someone objects that there's no silence around the word just now, that the noise is there, coming from Billy Graham and Jerry Falwell and all the other fundamentalists and revivalists and evangelicals, I have to say that I think the words "spirit" and "soul" and "repentance" and the like are debased by these strident and cocksure salesmen of the Lord and need to be rescued from them, in the same way that Chekhov once spoke of the theater needing to be rescued from "the hands of the grocers."

Anyway. How shall I put it? Something in me now and in the atmosphere, some dry element of inconsolable desire, an absence of satisfaction in the midst of abundance, the nearly total politicalization of our experience, its quantification too, accompanied by doubts, to be sure, but ones that have to do with functions and efficacies and not yet with true Doubt—all this has instigated this book.

No theologian, no philosopher or sage, only a sixty-one-year-old man with a smattering of learning and perhaps something of a style, a man to whom something happened long ago, has gained from one realm or other the courage to begin this enterprise, an undertaking that has appeared to him from the moment he decided on it to resemble too much the action and fate of the cartoon character who in pursuit or flight races past the edge of the cliff and is left furiously pedaling in empty space.

There had been a preamble, something being prepared, but at the time I couldn't have known it. So it all seemed to begin abruptly, without warning, on a very hot day in the summer of 1952. I was twenty-seven and didn't have a job at the time (my wife had a very small income, and since money went a long way in those days it was enough for us to live on) and so I spent my days mostly reading and going to the movies, art galleries and museums. I read eclectically and thought about things very much the same way. Without a specialty, professional or otherwise, or any organizing principle, I was like a child going helter-skelter through an encyclopedia.

The image is an apt one. When I was about ten or eleven my parents bought an encyclopedia for my sister and me. My father, a lawyer, never seemed to read anything but legal briefs and newspapers, while my mother was devoted to women's magazines like *The Ladies' Home Journal* and *Good Housekeeping* and to popular fiction, but my parents had the traditional Jewish concern for their children's intellectual propulsion, so I never lacked sympathy and encouragement during the wild spree of reading I embarked on as soon as I'd learned how—rather late, as it happened, at about seven.

I would read at all possible times but ritually, especially in the winter, between the hours of about four-thirty and six-thirty, or from the time I came inside after playing in the street until dinner. My favorite place was a corner of the living room between a sofa and the wall—a little reading cave I'd fashioned—and it was mostly there that I read the encyclopedia after it arrived (*Compton's Pictured Encyclopedia* it was called; how well I remember the dull-red nubbly covers), starting with A and going straight on to Z. In the course of this absurd enterprise I picked up such an abundance of marginal or useless information as to make me today a most formidable trivia-game player.

It's a snowy winter day, already dark, and I'm in my cave. The only sounds are some muffled noises from the kitchen. I'm two-thirds of the way through F and I turn a page. Then I'm stricken, ravished, seduced beyond hope of recovery. Across a double page is a huge title—"France: a Name that

33

Rings Like a Battle Cry!"—and below it is a photograph of an equestrian statue of Joan of Arc, the one at Rheims, the Maid in armor on a rearing horse, her hair cut in bangs, her lance held high, pointing to the heavens. My love affair with her, wholly without conscious erotic elements at its inception, and of course without religious elements either, began with these pages in the encyclopedia, along with my lifelong infatuation with France.

I wasn't what used to be called a "bookworm," nor was I in any way what we called then a "sissy," for I balanced my ferocious reading with equally ferocious participation in the urbanized sports we tirelessly played: stickball, punchball, roller hockey, stoopball, touch football and the rest. But I loved reading so passionately that my most powerfully sensuous memory from childhood is of an incident having to do with books.

I was nine or ten and was just getting over some serious illness, sufficiently recovered so that my parents thought it safe to leave me with my thirteen-year-old sister while they went for the evening to friends around the corner. The couple they were visiting had two sons a few years older than I, avid readers too, and the woman had told my mother she would give me the books they no longer wanted, which my mother promised me she'd bring back that night. I had a hard time falling asleep and when I woke early next morning saw nothing at first, so that my heart fell. But what had I expected? That my mother would cover me with the books or tie them to strings from the ceiling so that they would dangle over my face?

They were in a large carton on the floor by my bed and when I saw them I felt faint, dizzy with riches. I dumped the carton out on the bed and then lunged at the books, tossing them up in the air, running my hands through them like Silas Marner with his gold pieces, at last slowly and me-

thodically going through each one, noting its title and what
series it was part of (in those days nearly all books for boys,
for girls too, were written in series by astonishingly prolific
authors, some of whom, I later learned, wrote under five or
six pen names) and checking the illustrations. My favorite
series were all represented by at least several new titles: the
Rover Boys, The Hardy Boys, Bomba, the Jungle Boy, the
Boy Allies, Poppy Ott and Jerry Todd, Don Sturdy, Tom
Swift, Baseball Joe, the Mars books by Edgar Rice Bur-
roughs, the Ted Scott aviation series (I would never again
be as thrilled by any book's title as I was by two of those:
Lone Eagle of the Border and *Over the Rockies with the
Airmail*). Forty or fifty books, none of which I'd read.
Heaven.

But no matter how much I read, there were times when I
felt that it wasn't enough, that I needed longer, uninter-
rupted stretches. So for this reason, and surely other, unconscious, ones as well, I used to "arrange" little illnesses,
pretending to be sick or exaggerating trivial ailments in
order to be kept home from school for a few days (I never
did it on weekends or during vacations). Having gulled my
mother I would swiftly create a hermetic world on my bed,
the "Pleasant Land of Counterpane," as a Robert Louis Stevenson poem describes it. I would pile up on one side of me
the books and magazines (*Argosy* and *Doc Savage*) I intended to read and on the other a set of modeling clay, cray-
ons and paper, or cutouts, and would then be off on the most
delicious flight from responsibility and into imagination.
Until, rhythmically, a couple of days later I'd get itchy and
begin longing again for the physical tensions and releases of
outdoor games and sports.

I wasn't a good enough athlete to make any of the school
teams but I could hold my own in the informal games of the
neighborhood. Yet my interest in sports was so intense that

as soon as I got to high school, James Madison, I went out for the weekly paper as a sportswriter, was taken on and ended as sports editor in my senior year. At the University of Wisconsin I became an assistant sports editor on the *Daily Cardinal* and indeed until I went into the Marines in the latter part of World War Two my ambition remained that of writing about sports.

I was a good student, though not spectacular, nothing like my brilliant classmates such as Robert Solow, who's an eminent economist at MIT now, or Richmond Kotcher and Douglas Dukelsky (later Duke), both of whom must surely have become topnotch physicists or mathematicians. But for some reason I abruptly stopped reading, except for school, at about fifteen and only returned to my childhood passion at twenty, when the war, or my being in it and needing to oppose its world with imaginary ones, reawakened my hunger. For the next seven years, or until the time I was speaking of at the beginning of this section, I read as insatiably as I'd earlier done.

If anything distinguished my reading in 1952, when I was twenty-seven, it was the fact that it was all quite "elevated": avant-garde and classical fiction, poetry, literary criticism, history, philosophy, psychology and the like, but nothing in religion, toward which for years my attitude had been thoroughly skeptical, if not quite that of a belligerent atheist.

Pretty much an autodidact—the war had taken me from college in the middle of my junior year, and after I'd returned from more than three years in the Marines, one of them in the South Pacific, I'd barely finished a B.A. and taken a few desultory courses here and there—there had gradually formed in me an erratic and unsteady but discernible body of taste in art and predilections in ideas. For the most part my aesthetic values were strongly avant-garde and my intellectual appetite was for metaphysical and philosophical inquiry that might best be described as avant-garde too.

I had had a history of sudden ardent infatuations and temporary commitments to successive theories, movements, ideologies and individual writers. I'd been an amateur Marxist (which is to say I never joined any party), a Freudian, a D. H. Lawrentian (or Lawrenceite), by which I mean a feverish believer in that writer's sillier notions about "dark gods," the "wisdom of the blood" and the like.

(A few years before the time I'm speaking of I had spent a month in a little town on a lake near Guadalajara in Mexico, and had been overwhelmed to learn that Lawrence, that "skinny, redheaded, crazy Englishman," as the talkative, American-born proprietress remembered him, had twenty-five years or so earlier lived for a while in the same cottage I was occupying then. Maybe he had slept in the same bed? I couldn't bring myself to ask.)

Into all of these intellectual and literary amours, which had followed one another at intervals of a year or two and sometimes overlapped, I had plunged ecstatically, reading everything I could lay my hands on: a great deal of Marx, almost all of Engels and even three or four books of Lenin; everything that had been translated of Freud and Ernest Jones's three-volume biography; Lawrence down to the last obscure book, such as *Movements in European History*, which I had discovered with great excitement (since at the time it was supposed to be impossible to find) on a shelf in a remote dusty corner of one of the buildings of Foyle's on Charing Cross Road in London.

Proust was a continuing and inexhaustible love of mine. For a long time (and it hasn't changed all that much) I thought of *Remembrance of Things Past* in almost a religious way, insofar as it was a means for me, as it was for Proust, of transcending physical actuality and building a citadel against the onslaughts of time. Over the previous five or six years I had read the whole immense book twice in Scott-Moncrieff's English translation, the first time sitting day after day in a shellhole on the island of Peleliu in the South Pacific (before we sailed from San Diego I'd thrown out most of my socks and underwear to make room in my seabag for the two bulky volumes) and once, laboriously, with a dictionary at my side, in French.

I was preparing to be a writer but was much retarded in getting around to it. I had published nothing since my sports pieces in college except for a couple of poems that some editor thought were worth printing but that I knew were second-rate and derivative (of Yeats mostly), and had by now given up any thought of *being* a poet. I had dabbled in fiction—stories, schemes for novels, some of them quite elaborate—and had finally begun to write pieces, not criticism, not even real essays, but little passages of reflection, wandering insights from which I thought something might eventually grow.

I remember taking note around this time of the fact that Keats, to whom I otherwise wouldn't have dreamed of comparing myself, had been a year or two younger at his death than I was now. To say I was desperate about when I might begin a literary career would be putting it a little too strongly, but I was getting more and more anxious as the months and the years went by. I couldn't know then, and was not to begin to understand until several more years had passed, what was impeding me. Nor have I ever completely understood the relationship between my love of literature and ambition for it and the religious experience I was about to have.

There was another sort of dilemma, really a desperation, in which I was caught up, and this was a marriage that had been entered into too hastily and had been rather bad from the start but into which my wife and I were locked, by habit, fear and neurotic dependence. We had been together for four or five years and were now at a point of crisis. We had come together in the "liberated" atmosphere of Greenwich Village after the war, both of us dreaming of lives in the arts, both expectant, naive and half-formed. But intellectually we didn't have much in common and sexually we were ill-matched and mostly unhappy. She had gaps, I thought, in her capacity for both tenderness and arousal, her affliction being covered in my mind, as I remember that time now, by a word that was much more fashionable then than I gather it is now: "frigidity."

Yet pretty surely I was wrong. For I really knew very little about how and why women are aroused and, besides, whatever was true of my wife, the major part of our discordance came, I knew but hated to admit, from my own erotic nature and proclivities, what "turned me on," as we didn't then say.

On one side I was fervidly romantic, an idealizer and worshiper of women who was as dreamy about them and damply sentimental and quasi-mystical as the worst of the Pre-Raphaelites. I remember from my earliest youth thinking of women as "superior," charged with extraordinary spiritual power and so entrusted with rescue missions to the other, unfortunately coarser half of humanity. (But I never thought of the women of my own family this way; I was too embattled with them, too unconscious.)

And I remember always needing a "girlfriend," by which I meant, in that era of innocence when you didn't go out on dates until you were fifteen or older and sex at that age was unthinkable, someone I could admire and abstractly desire, who would put her gaze on me after selecting me from among all the *others*, and thereby grant me a precious *ap-*

proval; and who, it goes without saying, was more of a principle, a locus of my spiritual yearning, than a being or a body.

Once when I was about six I stole some extremely cheap costume jewelry from my sister's drawer to give to a classmate of mine, a girl named Doris, blond and pretty and, as I was able to see much later on, as vain and haughty as she could be. She accepted the things as her due but, to my heartbreak, showed me no greater favor than before. And all through that period of prepuberty when boys are known to turn away from girls, finding them silly and repulsive, I was the only one of my gang to hold out against the repudiation, maintaining a "relationship" with a girl named Leilah, whose books I carried home from school (oh, shades of Norman Rockwell!).

Then there was Miss Smith, the dark-haired, willowy, beautiful teacher under whose gentle guidance I learned to read, a gift from her so dazzling that, against the physical facts of the matter, I wished to make her my girlfriend too. And Helen, the young Polish girl who lived with us as our maid for several years when I was seven and eight. She was marvelous-looking, with the high Slavic cheekbones to which I was to become devoted, and she mothered me (not that my own mother was deficient in nurture; but caught, as I was dimly aware even then, in an unhappy marriage, she laid excessive psychic demands on me, her other "male"). When Helen went off to be married at twenty I was inconsolable, and did a bad job of hiding it.

Yet on the other side was my fear of women, a particular sort of fear that has always seemed to me to be much more like longing, or at least to have a great deal of confused and distraught desire connected to it. As I grew older I began to think of women—females—in one of my psychic conditions the way children think of roller coasters or spook tunnels:

the delicious swooning dangerousness of it. This sexual side of things was a "perversion," as I came to know through some book or other, officially one might say, after having suspected for some time that all wasn't well, that I wasn't "right."

I'm writing now from a nearly archaic moral outlook, a victim of the upraised fingers of forty years ago, and I sit here at the typewriter waiting for something to prod me into saying *it*. There finally comes to my rescue the memory of a story told to me by Theodor Reik, to whom I went some years ago for what turned out to be a largely unsuccessful analysis (he was very old and would fall asleep and I would wake him by coughing loudly).

One day I had suddenly stopped talking, out of embarrassment over the subject we were discussing, my sexual fantasies. The same thing had happened to him once during his analysis with Freud, he told me. He had been lying on the famous couch talking and had abruptly fallen silent. A minute or two had passed and then Freud had said, "Well?" "I can't go on," Reik had told him. "What's in my mind right now is so embarrassing. I'm ashamed of it." There was a pause and then Freud had said, "*Be* ashamed . . . but tell it."

And so I tell it. Although I was often enough "normal" in my sexual desires and activities and was potent most of the time, in some of my fundamental fantasies and cravings, which rose up and pressed me at intervals, I was a masochist. At least that was the category of perversion I had learned to apply to myself, after having read about it, I believe, in a book by Karen Horney, *The Neurotic Personality of Our Time* (which a friend of mine once transposed into *The Horny Personality of Our Time* by Karen Neurotic).

It's never taken the form of a wish to be whipped or burned with cigarettes or have hot wax dripped on me or

physically hurt in any way, but of being overpowered by
women larger and stronger (either physically or mentally
so) than myself and then being forced to submit to their desires. In fantasy and on the actual occasions I had managed
to create little scenarios or playlets, these desires essentially
had to do with cunnilingus, another word I'd become familiar with in my late teens.

I would have fantasies of amazonian women wrapping
their powerful thighs around my head or of women with
large buttocks sitting on my chest or face, imprisonments
from which I could only be released if I accepted my fate as
these women's sexual slave, although I didn't have the
slightest wish to be a slave in any other area.

To these ends I would cut out photographs of women
athletes from magazines and newspapers and of other
women with muscular or heavy (but not fat) legs, or sometimes the main enticement would be a cold "masterly" expression. These latter photos would be culled from the
quasi-pornographic magazines of the period. The women
would almost always be dressed in silk stockings, garter
belts and high heels, fetishistic items of attire from my earliest sexual memories, the preeminent icon being the famous
photograph of Marlene Dietrich as Lola Lola in *The Blue
Angel*, with her top hat, her languorous expression, her
hands clasped round her upraised knee, the mighty thigh
dazzling in its stocking and garters.

I had quite a collection of such pictures, which I kept in a
secret place (a problem, because our apartment was so
small) and "consulted" from time to time as aids to masturbation—something I didn't do all that often—or for simple
sensual reverie. Then one day my wife, who had participated rather perfunctorily and with some show of reluctance
in the "game playing" I would sometimes be able to arrange
between us, discovered my little erotic cache.

Her shock and disgust, which my own guiltiness prevented me from seeing as rather excessive, brought about a sharp rupture between us, but after a while we bridged it over and resumed our marriage on a fragile basis. Yet everything had changed. It was as though my time of innocence had run out, innocence meaning my idea that I could have a fantasy life entirely apart from others. Of course my wife knew something about my erotic dreams, but she hadn't known about the pictures and these, stimuli that left her out of account, naturally, or at least understandably, dismayed her. As long as I could keep the mild sadomasochistic games we played separate from my more wide-ranging fantasy life, I could struggle along between normality and abnormality, giving sufficient evidence of the former to make the latter almost invisible and therefore, I had thought, harmless.

From then on, with these things out in the open, the pictures remaining as a ground of suspicion between us, even though I made a big show of tearing them up, I was filled with alarm at the thought that our relationship might break up at any time. And this was despite the fact that it had never had much to sustain it, no real intellectual exchange, no deep companionship, and that our egos were always in competition. Later I would come to understand that our ties had been largely unconscious, displacements from primitive longings, and through that understanding be able to break away, as she became able to also.

The anxiety that held me and the despair I was in, not simply over the possibility of my marriage breaking up, of my being abandoned, as I saw it, but much more profoundly over my own nature, with its romantic idealization of women and the opposing force to that, the "illness" I felt to be a wide stain on my psychic being—all this doubtless played a part in what was about to happen.

My perversion, as I felt compelled to consider it, seemed to me to constitute a disqualification from ordinary, acceptable, "decent" existence, and this will surely be regarded by some readers as a more than adequate explanation of my conversion. I began to move toward religion perhaps a year or so after the incident with the photographs and, such readers will be likely to think, the facts I've just recounted are surely enough to account for that. But it was much more complex.

It will be said that because of the way I felt about myself I went to the Church for relief, protection, forgiveness or therapy; I had any number of such needs, to be sure, and they will figure in later. But what I have to insist on at this point is that I didn't *go* to the Church, it came to me. It pursued me. It? What? The hound of heaven is a metaphor, a poet's conceit. But something pursued me or, if that verb is too literal and anthropomorphic, something made me move, led me to act, directing my steps.

And I have to say too that my angst (another word I picked up in my early twenties) antedated my state of mind during the period I'm writing about and was wider than the particularities of my psychic life; it had to do with metaphysical matters, questions of ultimate existence, death and sentient foreclosure. Beyond this, I have to say something else, which is that when I did become a Catholic it became harder to live in many ways, not easier, and this was something I had suspected would be true. It would be false to pretend that once I'd been given an initial shove toward the Faith I hadn't some idea that I might find a point of peace within it, but never for a moment did I think of religion as a potential panacea, a radical "cure."

And beyond all this I have to repeat that one purpose of this book is my desire to look back at the time when the spiritual was a mode or level of existence for me, and that my own story, or history, was only a ground or occasion for the spiritual to show itself at work. There are other stories, other grounds, some of them no doubt psychologically or morally more extreme or peculiar than mine: murderers struck by the "light," Watergate conspirators fanning out on evangelical trails.

But religion, or the spiritual life, isn't made illegitimate and isn't "exposed" as fraudulent by the determination that there are psychological explanations for belief or the wish to believe; science, and even reason, has never had the last word in these matters and doesn't have it now. The point about the spiritual I both start with and want to inquire further into is that it isn't coterminous with the psychological, it isn't simply an archaic term for it. Something mysterious remains, something spills over. What this is may be a chimera in our present circumstances, it may, let's say, be parapsychological or the like, or it may be an ideal, which is to say unobtainable. But nothing of this is, or is ever likely to be, decided, and, as Pascal said, the heart, or the soul, continues to have reasons of which the mind is ignorant.

On the particular summer day I spoke of at the beginning of this section I remember waking up to a sense of boredom; I didn't have any ideas about the day nor plans of even the smallest kind. I muddled through the morning, fiddling with some scraps of writing, paying some bills, and then toward noon went to the bookshelves for something to read. Nothing appealed to me. At the time, not having much money and before the paperback revolution would come to my rescue, I didn't have a large collection of books of my own and so was an active user of the public library. So after lunch I walked over to Lexington Avenue from our tiny apartment on Seventy-ninth Street off Park and took the bus down to Fiftieth Street, where the Cathedral branch of the library was at the time.

I had seen the windows of this branch from the street but had never gone in and knew nothing about it. I usually went to a branch on Ninety-sixth near Lexington or to the main library at Forty-second and Fifth, but for some reason on that hot day I decided to try this other branch.

Inside the library I wandered among the aisles and browsed, with nothing particular in mind and growing more and more uncomfortable in the muggy heat. After an hour or so I had finally picked out five or six books. The only one of them I remember was a volume of the letters of Hart Crane, whose opaque poetry I had been reading, although I think there may have been an early novel of Evelyn Waugh's, maybe *Decline and Fall*. Anyway, I put them all under my arm and started to walk toward the checkout counter.

I had taken the last book from a shelf perhaps twenty feet from the desk, and before I could get halfway there something came over me or took hold of me—this is the only way I can describe what happened—some impulse made me turn back, hesitate, and then walk over to a section of the library, an alcove on the far side of the checkout counter, where I hadn't been before.

It was quite separate from the main part of the library and could easily be overlooked. There were maybe a thousand books on its shelves and when I got there and began to glance over the titles I could see that the books were all concerned in one way or another with religion. They were divided into a general section and then into the various faiths, a section on Judaism, one on Islamism, another on Catholicism, and so on.

There's nothing here that could possibly interest me, I remember telling myself. I had an aversion to religious books and even to ones *about* religion, and so never read any. Yet as I write this I suddenly recall that there had been an exception to this informal taboo, the circumstances of which seem worth interrupting my narrative chronology to recount.

A year earlier my wife and I had gone to Europe for the first time. On the boat—a charming old French liner called the *DeGrasse*—we had become friendly with a French family, a couple in their thirties and their two daughters, who were about eight and nine. Their name was Weil, and when I asked if they were related to Simone Weil, about whom I had vaguely heard (she was just becoming known in America, some years after her death), the man, André, who I would later discover was a famous mathematician, told me, with an odd touch of reluctance or embarrassment, I thought, that he was her brother.

I became infatuated with the girls, Sylvie and Nicolette, and their pleased mother, Eveline, invited me to visit them when we got to Paris. I went to their rambling old apartment on the Rue August-Comte behind the Luxembourg Gardens, where Eveline showed me some of Simone's books and papers. Then I took the girls to the gardens for the Punch-and-Judy show and other divertissements, after which I bought them ice cream, a ritual we repeated three or four times over the following weeks.

Back home that fall I found out as much as I could about Simone and read her book, *Waiting for God*, which had recently been translated. I remember having been greatly moved by the life and mind of this brilliant, unclassifiable young woman, politically radical, intellectually rigorous, who, a Jew, had hovered for so long at the door of the Catholic Church and had died, in an extraordinarily sacrificial way, without having become able to go in.

Yet I'd also been discomfited by the book and what I'd learned of her life, unable to accommodate the specifically spiritual elements, seeing her religious hunger as eccentric if not pathological. Only after my own movement into the Church did I go back to her, avidly reading her books as they posthumously appeared, being stirred all over again and coming to regard her as a precursor whose spirituality dwarfed my own yet offered me exemplary hints and a certain solace.

To return to that summer day in 1952. Turning around, I started to walk back to the checkout counter. But I'd taken only a few steps when once again something prevented me from going on, stopping me in midstride and making me go back to the alcove. Once more, this time very much against my will, I began to look over the books, which I did without at first really seeing any of them.

After a while, the eerie pressure continuing to rise, I took one or two off the shelves—I remember some such title as *A History of Islam*—with my state of mind changing from bafflement to growing irritation at what was happening. A second time I started to leave the alcove and a second time I was impelled back to it as though by an unseen hand pressing me gently but authoritatively between my shoulder blades.

This time I found myself standing in front of the section of books on Catholicism. My annoyance continuing to mount, feeling also a prickle of disgust, even a touch of nausea, I ran my eyes over the books. I've said it was hot and I remember now that the sweat was pouring from my forehead, so that with the pile of books I'd picked out before under one arm I had to wipe my brow with my other forearm. I stood there for a moment with my eyes closed, until I finally opened them and began really to look at the shelves. I noticed some lives of saints, a type of being about which I

had very little knowledge and a great deal of dis
some books by Cardinal Newman, of whom I had
couldn't place.

Then, standing there and literally struggling in the grip of
the same insistent force whose pressure I'd felt from the
outset of this weird experience, wondering if the dozen or so
other people in the library were noticing anything, since I
knew that I was trembling and scraping my shoes on the
floor in an effort to turn round and get away—a kind of
clown act or demented dance movement it might have
seemed to an onlooker—I finally found myself reaching for a
book and taking it off the shelf.

The book I'd taken down was called *The Spirit of Medieval Philosophy* and was by someone I'd never heard of, a
man named Etienne Gilson. When I looked at the jacket
blurb pasted on the inside of the front cover, the way library
books often have them, I learned that he was a French philosopher, an authority on Saint Thomas Aquinas who had
been teaching at some university in Canada. (Later I was to
note the similarity of his last name to mine, but not make
anything of it.)

The book was a big one, a real tome, and as I reluctantly
leafed through it, turning the pages with an effort and forc-
ing myself to read a few lines here and there, it struck me as
dry, technical, full of alien language and ideas . . . as much as
I could make out of those. In any case it was nothing in
which I could conceivably have any interest, I told myself.

So I put it back on the shelf, picked up the books I'd chosen before, turned around, found myself without any power
to move, turned back again, took the Gilson book from the
shelf once more, put it back, repeated the whole mad cycle
three or four more times and then, besieged, light-headed as
though I had a fever, nearly sick to my stomach, put the
book with my others and, muttering to myself something to

the effect of "if the only goddamned way I can get the hell out of this goddamned fucking place is to take out this fucking goddamned book, then I'll just have to do it," went over to the counter, checked out all the books and walked out of the library into the glaring sunlight.

I got into an uptown Lexington Avenue bus (the avenue was two ways at the time) and sat down near the back of the bus with the books in my lap. I put the Gilson book on the top of the pile and kept staring at the cover, which was a dull red color, as I remember, while my annoyance kept growing. It was stifling in the bus, so I reached to open a window. After fumbling with it for a while and finally getting it open I had a sudden, nearly irresistible wish to fling the Gilson book out into the street, and went so far as to pick the book up from the seat and hold my arm out the window with it barely held in my grasp. For nearly a minute I fought the urge to drop it, shaking with tension, until my practical sense took over with the realization that I could ill afford to pay for what was clearly an expensive volume. So I brought my arm back in and, feeling strangely ill and exhausted, sat back and rode on to my stop.

That afternoon I read one of the books I'd brought home, a short novel I think it was, leafed through the Hart Crane letters and then, toward suppertime, found myself (I can't emphasize too strongly how in everything I've been describing and in nearly all the events that are to follow I kept "finding" myself in certain places or situations or doing certain things, not deliberately or even consciously choosing to be there or to do them), I found myself, as I say, toying with the Gilson book once again. I kept picking it up and putting it down, turning to something else and then picking it up again. Once I put it on a high shelf so as to get it out of my immediate reach.

But then, after an hour or two of this nonsense, in obedience to the same sort of spooky dictate I had felt in the library, I began to page reluctantly through it. After a few minutes of this I became aware that I wasn't going to get away so easily and so, with a shrug of acceptance of what I certainly didn't think of at the time as any sort of supernatural influence but, I remember thinking before I started, some temporarily mysterious unconscious prompting that would eventually be wholly explicable, I settled down to read the book.

It was hard going at first, as I'd expected, but very soon the difficulties dwindled and then vanished. To find myself caught up in this unprepossessing book couldn't have been more astonishing to me, but that was how it was. Very quickly I forgot the strange circumstances that had brought the book to me, or me to it, so that it very soon seemed as if it were the most natural thing in the world for me to be reading it.

What was most astounding was the effortlessness with which I was carried along. I had had some minimal training in philosophy (and not a bit in theology), an introductory course or two at Wisconsin and one on the Greeks at the New School after the war, and I'd supplemented that with some scattered, disorganized reading in Plato, Schopenhauer, Nietzsche, and the like, for the most part philosophers whom I considered to be more "writers," artists, than abstract thinkers or builders of systems. And so I was far from having the schooled, supple background and cast of mind such a book as this would seem to have required.

Yet I found myself following with nearly complete ease Gilson's intricate arguments and explications, all of them laid out with much heavy technical diction and with many references to works and ideas and figures I'd known nothing about. It was as though I'd suddenly and unaccountably been gifted with a great clarity of mind and speed of understanding, a lucidity such as I never imagined I could possess and which, to be sure, I was never again to enjoy to anything like the same degree.

I read on through the evening and into the night in the silent apartment (my wife was out of town), having a bite of supper which I ate with the book propped up on the table in front of me, keeping myself going later with numerous cups of coffee, smoking furiously, taking numerous notes, marking passage after passage, finally toward dawn dropping down on the sofa in my clothes for a few hours of sleep. When I woke up I grabbed the book and started reading again. I read through breakfast, a thin lunch, a thinner supper and on into the evening. At last, about one or two in the morning, I think it was, exhausted, my head swimming yet with a point of hard clear light at the center of my consciousness, I turned the last page (of 400, 500, more?), made my final notation, put the book down and said, aloud, to myself and to the air, in a voice that didn't sound like mine at all, feeling a little self-conscious as I did it, something like this: "It's true, all of it, it's all true."

True. Not beautiful or exciting or comforting, which were in fact qualities I associated with the experience soon afterward but weren't what I was thinking when I finished the book. True. I find it nearly impossible to explain or even describe what I mean by this, but I owe it to you to try.

It was as if what I had read during that day and a half had established an intellectual or philosophical world as solid and factual as the physical universe, as if the claims and arguments Gilson had made weren't claims and arguments at all but statements of what was actually so. I imagine that mathematicians and physicists have this extraordinary sense, when they've completed a proof or a demonstration, that something new exists now, not just in their minds but in reality. What now existed for me against all previous likelihood, all plausibility, was the Catholic religion, the arguments for whose truth had been made irrefutable for me during this long stretch of reading. Irrefutable, the way a rock is or the ocean. What hadn't existed for me before I read the book now did.

I can remember almost nothing of what Gilson wrote; all I can recall was a voice, a tone, a sense of authority, and my physical condition at the time: feverish, sweating, my back aching more and more, my eyes half-ruined. And I can remember some vague details of the apartment's decor: its austerity, which derived as much from lack of wherewithal as from taste; the rough bookshelves, a pile of records in a corner.

But I knew that the book wasn't in any way directly aimed at conversions, mine or anybody else's. It wasn't remotely an evangelical tract but a complex, difficult work of logic and rationality. At the time it seemed to me the most extraordinary product of rational thinking I'd ever come upon; it was unassailable and not to be resisted. Later I would read various other formal arguments for the existence of God, the divinity of Christ and the legitimacy of the Catholic claim to be the one true Church (almost all of which arguments or "proofs" I've forgotten), but after *The Spirit of Medieval Philosophy* I needed no further intellectual persuasion.

This morning I looked over the notes I wrote out the day after I finished reading the book. There are some thirty-five or forty pages, closely typed, which I filled with sentences and passages from the book, together with a number of comments of my own. I had to rummage for these notes and finally pulled them out of an old loose-leaf notebook filled with quotes from a great many other books of all sorts and stuck away for years with other odds and ends of my intellectual and personal history in a cardboard carton I found sitting in the latest of various dark closets.

At first as I read through them it all seemed entirely strange, as if the writing were in an unknown or dead language:

> For the human soul is act, and is therefore a thing for itself and a substance; the body, on the contrary, although without it the soul cannot develop the fullness of its actuality, has neither actuality nor subsistence, save those received from its form, that is to say the soul.

> Nothing contingent can be a necessary and natural object for the divine intellect. Not its necessary object; since the sole necessary object is the divine essence: nor its natural object, since it acquires the character of object only in virtue of a voluntary decision. But then also conversely, no created intellect can have God for natural object, for if there is no natural relation between the creature and God, neither can there be between God and the creature.

At first I found it almost impossible to believe that these passages, so wholly abstract, so much like jets of colorless gas or mathematical markings, that these sentences should have meant so much to me when I first read them, should have been so convincing. (To be fair to Gilson, he wasn't always as dry and abstract as this; at times he could be an eloquent writer, even in a theological vein.) But as I turned from the typewriter and went through the notes again something began to change.

To begin with, I started to recover some traces of the edge and flavor of that humid day and night, two nights, so long ago when I sat reading voraciously, and felt myself making my way through a dense forest all of whose vegetation parted at my approach. For those hours I was fervid with intellect, moving steadily through a corridor of light, entirely light myself, weightless in a realm where everything held together, where the rendings and oppositions of the truths of our lives seemed overcome and healed. I remember a line from a letter Columbus wrote to Queen Isabella from the New World: "I have discovered many beautiful islands where the birds sing all day." It was like that for a moment for me then, and one impulse behind this book is perhaps a wish to have it somewhat like that again. I don't mean that I'm hoping or planning to recover the truths I saw and accepted then; my intention isn't in any way to regain the Faith, to "believe" again.

But what I do hope for is to regain some of the understanding I had at that time, the substance of which has become frayed and raveled in the years that have passed and by now has almost disappeared. And in reading through the notes, I find, with excitement, that an intellectual core or framework comes back into view, that the gist of what Gilson wrote and I assented to is within my grasp again. I've had to brush away a tear. For it seems to me that ideas and intellectual convictions we once held but that have changed or vanished retain their life in a certain way; like emotions that have altered or receded, they remain as part of the archives of the self. We are always in part what we were.

As I go through the notes I see that the central elements in my having been won over were almost entirely philosophical and intellectual, which is in the first place to say that they had nothing to do with the type of conversion experience that is said to spring from a physical vision—of Jesus, God the Father, or whatever—and is almost always accompanied by a powerful feeling of repentance, the sinner contemplating his or her black heart and resolving to mend his or her ways. There was no "presence" for me, no "voice," no "light," only that of the intellect. I didn't fall to my knees in worship, I didn't call out "Lord! Lord!" nor did I think about my sins. I wasn't morally transformed at all.

What happened, as nearly as I can put it, was that I saw the world in a new way, saw explanations where there had been frustrating mysteries and alluring mysteries where there had been unsatisfying explanations. I finished the book with a double sight, as of two realms; one was of material, psychological, physical and social life, the other was of transcendence, a dominion of ultimates, the ground on which everything "actual" rested. The view of existence Gilson was explicating, essentially that of Saint Thomas and Saint Augustine, along with other medieval philosophers like Duns Scotus, took shape in my mind as "truth."

"Why should there be anything rather than nothing?" Leibniz had asked, to which question, one that had tormented me for years, Gilson's book is initially addressed. In reading over my notes I've jotted down a number of words or headings that among them sum up his central arguments and theses: necessity, Creation, God as Being and as the Word, a personal God, individuation, free will, sin, love, grace. Of these the first several were most decisive for me and I can best render what the ideas they represented meant to me by quoting from the Latin, as Gilson does, the sentence from which everything else flowed: "Ego sum qui sum—I am who am."

In this philosophical perspective God is "the pure act of existing . . . He has no cause; He himself is cause." "We might possibly not exist," Gilson goes on, but God cannot not exist. It follows from this, or did for me then, that "He is necessarily eternal because existence is His essence," and it follows too that, through an act of His love, we might share in eternity. "Christianity," Gilson writes in a sentence that moved me more than any other, "put the end of man beyond the limits of this earthly existence."

Though I understood at the time that if I were to become a Catholic my moral and psychic condition would surely figure in crucially, that wasn't uppermost in my mind at the time. This first stage in my conversion—for that's all it proved to be—had accomplished a most significant change in my thinking: for the first time I saw the supernatural as real, not a myth, not a human construction out of longing, and this was the source of both my excitement and initial "belief." I see now too that the idea of God as the Word, Logos, was especially seductive, since I'd lived by words, craving them, struggling with them and trying to bend them to my poor aspiring uses for so long. I had been, in short, commandeered wholly through the mind, and any revolution of the entire self, any transformation of the spirit, would have to wait.

It's now the summer of 1953. Once more I find myself in the Cathedral branch of the public library, standing again in that alcove of books on religion, but this time as a result of my own decision. I choose among other books something called *The Seven Storey Mountain*, which is by Thomas Merton, a Trappist monk who was also a poet; I'd read a poem or two of his before. At home I begin to read his account of his conversion to Catholicism from what he described as nonbelieving Protestantism.

From the beginning I find the book extremely interesting, though I'm far from being overwhelmed by it. It's literate and shrewd, though there are some self-indulgent notes in it and a strain of contempt for the secular world that strikes me as rather mean-spirited. But then I come to a section that sends my brain into a whirl, so that I have to lie down on the bed to recover.

Merton is describing a summer day (in the early forties, I think it was) when, bored and restless, with nothing in his apartment he wants to read, he decides to go to the Cathedral branch of the library and takes the Lexington Avenue bus down. He is about the same age as I was at the time of my adventure there. He had studied at Columbia, where he had been active in literary affairs, and he has the same greedy appetite for books and ideas as I've had, although he is considerably further along in a literary career. And he has the same hostility to religion, organized or not.

In the library he picks out a number of books and gets ready to leave. After much hesitation and shuffling about he finds himself, against his conscious intention, taking Gilson's *Spirit of Medieval Philosophy* from the shelf and checking it out with his other books. Then he gets into a Lexington Avenue bus to go home.

Riding along he stares at the Gilson book and then has a furious impulse to throw it out the window. But he resists the urge out of a consideration of his poverty. At home he reluctantly finds himself reading the book, stays with it for a very long stretch of hours until he finishes it, and when he finally puts it down is completely convinced.

A couple of years after my baptism I wrote to Merton, who was by then steadily gaining in reputation as a poet and religious figure. (His name at the Trappist monastery in Kentucky was Father Louis.) To my hectic letter, filled with astonishment and pleading for his thoughts on the matter, he replied, laconically I'd say, "Such are the ways of the Lord."

Yes, indeed, such are the ways, and who can credit them? It's quite possible that one reason for my long hesitation about writing this book was that I suspected that my story about the library and the Gilson book, and then on top of that Merton's story and after that some other bizarre events, would be more than people would accept, that the incidents would be greeted with derision or at the very least profound skepticism (there's just as much chance of that happening now, of course). If the events were to be believed at all they would be subjected to any number of theories, almost all of them psychological explanations of one kind or another, which was the way I myself wished and tried to interpret them at the time.

I say "tried to" because I found it impossible to get round the great mysteriousness of the affair, no matter what line of possibility I pursued. But beyond this, by the time I read the Merton book, which I suppose I have to say again I hadn't heard of before, much less read (a friend once suggested that the crucial section might have been communicated to me tele-pathically!), enough events of a similar kind had occurred to carry me far past any sort of reasonable, natural explanation.

Gilson's book had convinced me, but what did that mean? After the first swaying of my mind, the thrilling recognition of truth and the lovely sense that this was what I had been looking for intellectually all along, the conviction quickly became abstract and aloof, like a set of proofs in algebra or physics, and remained that way for some time. I could see now how mystery and reason might be reconciled, and how there could be such a thing as supernatural truth and a personal God. I "believed," yet it wasn't as a believer, anyone I recognized as such. All that my belief meant to me at the time was that I could give a tight dry nod of assent in the direction of ideas and propositions that all my previous conscious life had been unthinkable. Something like a catching of my breath took place whenever I tried to look at the world in the way I had always done before. But I couldn't move, couldn't act; in reading over the notes I took from Gilson I come upon a sentence that describes what I felt about this paralysis: "What does it avail to know the good without power to put it into practice?"

Years later I would read Kierkegaard on the subject (on my way out of the Church, as it happened) and would learn in retrospect about the condition I had been in. Somewhere Kierkegaard had written this: "In case I really have a conviction (which is, after all, a determination in inwardness in the direction of the spirit), my conviction always has a higher value to me than the reasons on which it is grounded. In actuality, it is the conviction which *bears* the reasons, not the reasons which bear the conviction." I could see from what Kierkegaard said that I didn't really have a conviction—by definition a conviction makes you act—but was simply standing there holding a bunch of reasons.

But it was much more difficult than that. To accept, as I had so suddenly and unaccountably come to do, that God truly existed, that Christ was divine (I never for a moment thought of Christ as simply a "good man"; either He was God or He was a liar), and that the Catholic Church rested on these truths and was their trustee and interpreter, all this left me powerless to act.

When I thought of all the implications, especially everything that related to the Church, I was swiftly thrown into a turbulence in which instinctive horror at the notion of joining the enemy, the vaguely menacing Gentiles or goyim of my youth, of already in a sense having joined them, mingled with alarm, amounting to terror, at the prospect of *being* a Catholic in practice, having to do what's required of a Catholic, about which at first I didn't have the faintest idea, except that I suspected it must be pretty unpleasant. For a time after I read the Merton book, for example, I had periodic bouts of dread that I too would have to become a monk, in order to fulfill some mystical plan. (Later I'll describe one such occasion.)

So I quickly began to devise or, more accurately, there half-consciously took shape in me a protective strategy against the distressing summons, a summons that seemed implicitly to follow on my having accepted a body of thought and assertion about what was true at the heart of things. Most useful to this scheme of protection was a fact I soon seized on, that Gilson had been writing about the distant past, about a system of belief that had flourished most widely, normative and mostly unchallenged, six or seven hundred years ago.

This made it possible for me to introduce into my "certainty" a sly note of doubt, not about the spiritual or intellectual truths themselves but about what I might call their historical situation and thus their relation to me. Was there any connection, I asked myself, between the reality Gilson had been writing about, medieval Catholicism and its ethos, its soul one might say, and the Church I knew something about now? My sense of the present-day Church was made up of some odds and ends of factual information such as any educated person would be likely to have, but much more fully of impressions of a cloudy kind, as well as of bias and rumor, reflexive distaste and a number of strands of fear.

Everything I thought I knew about contemporary Catholicism tended to fill me with contempt: its intellectual narrowness, its hostility to new ideas, and especially its enmity toward all that I valued in present-day art and literature. Against this, even though I knew something about the corruptions and debasements of the earlier Church—anyone with the slightest historical sense couldn't fail to—it continued to hold an attraction for me.

To start with, again like any educated person, I had responded to its still powerful visual presence, everything that remained from the time when it had been the locus of physical beauty. I had prowled through cathedral after cathedral in France, Italy and Spain and had spent a lot of time in the museums. But more than that, I knew that there had been a time when whatever there was to know about life, nature, the way things worked, was known there, within the

Church's walls. You had to respect that, to put it mildly.

Against this the present Church seemed to me pinched, blind and joyless; it gave off an atmosphere of sullen ignorance, of meanness precisely in the realm of the spirit. Could the truths I'd accepted so eagerly have flown off sometime during the centuries that had intervened between Saint Francis of Assisi or even Saint Teresa of Ávila and the age of Father Coughlin and the glinting wire spectacles of Pius XII? Were those truths hovering somewhere up in the spiritual stratosphere now? I couldn't imagine them alive in the institution that claimed always to have sheltered and proclaimed them.

Along with this my intellectual conversion, or what I referred to for some time as my "abstract" conversion, couldn't at first put up any resistance at all to my general psychic history and conditions of temperament. By this I mean principally my aversion to joining any formal group and the dislike I felt, shared by my generation and by every new generation to a degree, for authority and for codes of morality, though a *way* of being moral was something I realized I'd been looking for through all the years, and is something I'll naturally return to later in this book.

More than anything else, beyond even the "objective" grounds I considered I had for shunning the Church whose teachings I had theoretically accepted, these new beliefs were helpless against the reign of their names and words in my head, the way "Catholic" and "priest" and "Calvary," "nun," "mortal sin," "Vatican" and the rest moved or sat as presences in my mind. For from my first memories of any of these words having been there—at the age of five? six? for some of them—they had been alien, dismal and distressing.

To my family, words like "Catholic" and "goy" and "priest" had of course been alien and threatening too. And now I remembered something I'd long forgotten, a time in my early adolescence when my father seemed to have betrayed us by giving up the fear and detestation we were all tacitly supposed to feel. He had become a fan of Father Coughlin.

My father was a dour, straitlaced "Yankee Jew" (as I afterward came to think of him). He had been born and raised in Connecticut, was a newsboy and pinball setter in his youth, about whose rigors he would never fail to remind me when I asked him for a dime or a quarter, and a graduate of Fordham Law School. He was a devoted reader of the *New York Sun*, which was all stock market reports and grumpy politics, and, an ardent Republican, was the only man in our Jewish middle-class neighborhood in Brooklyn who wore Alf Landon's sunflower in his lapel in 1936.

I remembered now how, to my dim alarm, he would listen unfailingly on Sunday afternoons to the radio preacher from Michigan, a look of approbation on his face which only faded when Coughlin began to add directly anti-Semitic outbursts to his tirades against Roosevelt, the plutocrats and the money changers. So "Father Coughlin" was among the names that lay darkly in my head.

In my imagination these words gave off an odor, had a certain dominant color and comprised some sort of shape. Understandably the color was black, superficially of course from the clothing of the priests and nuns I would see from time to time, as well as the hearses and coffins I associated with the church in the neighborhood where I grew up, far more than I connected them with the local synagogue, from which surely as many people were habitually buried. But it derived from something else too, something I can only call the darkness of the inimical.

The basis of this, understandably, was my Jewishness. Against us, against *me*, Gentiles had always been ranged, inexplicably to me when I was very young, then in a stance of enmity that at least offered allegations about us to give it a basis outside "motiveless malignity." We were this, we were that; we were criminal, tainted, low. But anti-Semitism doesn't account for all the darkness that I saw. Christians, Catholics, were inimical to me beyond what they thought of us or had done to us; they were, on that level of irrational response I've been talking about, figures of harm and negation in themselves. I hated their practices, such as I knew of them, above all the way they seemed to esteem death instead of fleeing from it—I remembered with horror the Falangist, hence Catholic, general in the Spanish Civil War whose toast was "Long live death!"—their iconography of blood and wounds.

The odor, which had to be metaphorical in its origin since I had never been in a church until I was twenty-five (I went to Notre Dame on one of my first days in Paris), I can only describe as a sort of mustiness compounded of dust and rectitude, which I would later replace with the sickly sweet smell of actual incense. And the shape, which had nothing to do with real structures, was of something squat, square, full of heaviness. Rather like the Merchandise Mart in Chicago, as a matter of fact, this shape implied that it might at any moment start moving to crush you; its massive institutionality flattened any sense of self. Such an image was of course as far as anything could be from that of Chartres, where you could be lifted up with the soaring.

All in all a dark, musty, brutal heaviness, repellent, existing only at the edges of my consciousness but powerful there. Long after I had become a Catholic traces of that original sense of the Church remained in me.

And then there were Catholics, real people. The Flatbush section of Brooklyn where I grew up was a heavily Jewish middle-class neighborhood. There was only a sprinkling of Catholic families in the several streets, or "blocks" as we called them, where I lived as a child and youth, with somewhat greater concentrations of them at the edge of the district. Beyond that lay *their* region, another country, enemy territory we thought of it, although there was very little actual violence of a racial or religious kind.

Almost all the Catholics I knew or knew about were Irish or Italian (nearly every one of my grade-school teachers was an Irish spinster), together with a handful of people with Slavic- or Russian-sounding names who were most likely Polish. If there were any Protestants, I didn't know about them; for years the word "Protestant" suggested to me a special, minor, pallid kind of Catholic.

In such a neighborhood I never experienced any direct anti-Semitism, no "kike" or "Christ killer" was ever hurled at me by swarthy or redheaded boys. But inevitably from the beginning of my conscious life and increasingly as I got older, hints would reach me from the world beyond our physically and socially comfortable ghetto, which never thought of itself as one. I would hear my parents, and with particular discomfort my grandparents, on whose lips the words had the sound of a curse, speak of "them," the "goyim" and the "Gentiles."

Always their tone of voice and the references they made indicated to me that in some way I didn't at all understand "they" were our enemies. Later the events of the thirties—Hitler and the Nazis, anti-Semitic movements in this country—gave this enemy clearer faces and specific names. But the Gentiles from whom the hatred and danger were said to flow were for a long time an indistinct crowd in my mind, a dim community, or rather "horde," for which I'd use the word "Catholic" as often as I did "Christian."

In actuality it was the Catholic kids on the block and in school who were the "different" ones, the minority whom we thought of as being in some ill-defined way inferior to us.

65

This sense of our superiority, subtly inculcated at home and in the streets, was no doubt due as much to ethnic and class attitudes (the Catholic men were much more likely to be proletarian or at any rate less educated than the Jews, who were lawyers, as my father was, doctors, dentists, druggists, storekeepers or owners of small businesses) as to religious ones.

Still, we didn't really separate those things. There was an indefinable aura that came from the fact that these people weren't Jewish. It would hang over the homes of the Irish and Italian families, most of whom lived in two-family houses that were physically indistinguishable from our own. I remember how I would walk by these houses with a side-long glance as at something vaguely mysterious, slightly tainted, not "right." It couldn't have occurred to me that this was exactly the way Christians looked at houses where Jews lived, in American small towns and even in sections of New York.

There were two or three Irish and Italian boys who participated in our games and sports, but none with whom I had any degree of friendship, none whose home I would ever visit or whom I would invite to my house. (I remember that when my sister as a teenager became close friends with an Italian girl in the neighborhood my parents regarded it as odd if not alarming.)

It wasn't in fact until after I had read the Gilson book that I would enter into a relationship with anyone Catholic, by which I mean a relationship where the other person's Catholicism figured as something active and recognized between us, as my being Jewish figured too. Before that, when I was in high school and college and the Marines, I'd known Catholics to be sure, but our respective religious backgrounds weren't things to be intelligently considered; they were incidental facts of difference such as we're taught in our democracy, at least genteel and respectable people are, either to make light of or rigorously suppress.

This, then, was my history and those my attitudes when, a couple of months after the Night of the Book, as I'd taken to calling it, I felt the first stirrings of desire to slow down in my headlong flight from the heavenly hound, whose spiritual fangs, to stay within the conceits of Thompson's poem, had been keeping me in such close range. I knew I couldn't remain indefinitely in the purely intellectual realm I had been inhabiting, nor could I turn back from it to what now would have been "prehistoric."

So I began to act, in the only way that seemed possible to me at the time. I began to read books like Cardinal Newman's *Apologia pro Vita Sua*, and some lives of the saints, none of which was very helpful to me at that stage, and to go into Catholic churches, surreptitiously and at odd hours— early in the morning or at lunchtime, once in a while in the evening. The secretiveness wasn't so much due to a fear of someone seeing me, some friend, say, as to a great reluctance to "seeing" myself in the act of going through those doors. So I played a strange game.

Once inside, I would slump down in one of the rearmost pews and peer, in effect through my fingers, at the scene before me, the furnishings, the altar, the pews and whatever people might be there for prayer or any other purpose. I remember staring almost unseeingly at a priest or altar boy making preparations for Mass, which I would never stay to watch. I remember looking at people, almost always elderly women, lighting votive candles, although I didn't know at the time that they were called that. I was this person, this voyeur, and at the same time I was the distant, critical yet violently agitated consciousness which refused to acknowledge that I was really, physically there. The tension was so great at first that I couldn't bear it for long and would turn and run out, sometimes having barely stepped inside.

But as the weeks went by I found myself gradually becoming able to stay for longer periods and to open my eyes and really look around. But when I was able to take in what I saw in those neighborhood churches I went to, it was enough to make me want to rush right out again.

I would look around, take things in and then become almost giddy with revulsion. The drab and the gaudy, blows to the eye from opposite directions. The stained-glass windows that seemed to have been put together from numbered kits. The hideous paintings "in the manner of": saints in whose faces and postures medieval or Renaissance ecstasy or anguish have been trivialized into simperings or pouts; cosmeticized Christs or ones the color of flounders' bellies. The Sacred Hearts that filled me with loathing for their medical or anatomical details, their idiotic literalness. The gilt, the gewgaws, the excrescences without visual or thematic point.

Banality everywhere, bad taste raised to a principle, to a credo: a God of bad taste? Was it possible? For it all seemed believed in, *willed;* it couldn't, I thought, have come about simply through a kind of infectious failure of skill and imagination. My most charitable interpretation of what lay behind the ugliness was that every aspect of physical or artistic reality in these buildings had to be degraded so that the spiritual realm might assert its claims more forcefully. After all, transcendence pointed above and beyond the material world, so whoever was in charge, or the committee mind in its calculations, had to be careful not to allow the material domain to display itself too alluringly. Still, they hadn't thought that way in Europe at one time. . . .

There was another related atmosphere and presence in the

churches I would go to, one that was not so much ugly as dreary and dispiriting. It rose from the people I saw, the scattered forms kneeling in prayer or lighting candles or simply sitting and staring at the altar. Because I never went to what one could think of as an "upper-class" church, never went on Sundays or at any time when there was a Mass or a funeral or any other formal activity or ceremony, the people I would see seemed to me to make up no sort of congregation, no community of believers. I didn't know what I wanted them to be, except that I understood that in some central way I was judging the Faith by them, and as it was, they struck me as a haphazard, shifting, lumpen group of transients, a silent rabble.

In the early morning they were most likely to be charwomen, dumpy European figures in long heavy skirts and babushkas, or watchmen, hotel clerks or doormen coming off duty and others from the occupational margins of the night. At lunchtime, when I would sometimes go to small midtown churches and, once or twice, when I found myself there on some business or other, to churches in the City Hall and Wall Street areas, and once on the Lower East Side, they were most often shopgirls or secretaries or Irish-looking men in gray suits and snap-brim fedoras, FBI types, graduates of Fordham Law. I thought it impossible that I could ever be able to address my prayers to the same god as they did, could ever crowd with them for comfort under the same celestial wing.

A few years later I would read Paul Claudel's account of how after he had returned to the Church following a period of rebellion from it he went one morning to an early Mass at Notre Dame and was appalled by his fellow worshipers, most of whom were washerwomen, prostitutes, night porters and the like. And then he had been dismayed to discover his lip curling in disdain. He examined himself, he tells us, and came to understand, with as much feeling as that granitic poet-statesman would allow himself to express in such a confession, that the Church had to embrace all social classes, that it would be monstrous if it didn't regard its members as equal, at least within its own precincts.

My own snobbery, which was never quite extinguished and which at certain periods was subtly altered into a form of condescension, didn't come to diminish gradually at this time through a growing process of tolerance or a self-instruction in humility like Claudel's, but went down sharply as a result of two encounters I was about to have. For the first time I would enter the presence of Catholics in an intimate, unguarded way, so that there might be a face to a face, a voice to a voice.

I often used to walk past a little lending library and information center attached to a church in my neighborhood, St. Ignatius Loyola (though at the time I didn't know who *he* was). It happened to be on Park Avenue and was therefore presumably one of those more or less upper-class churches of the kind I had deliberately avoided. I'm not at all sure why I did this, except that it had something to do with my idea, picked up from casual reading and rumor, that the institutional Church was fat with money and was an economic oppressor and I didn't want to get any direct evidence for that. A silly, confused notion, but so were a lot of my ideas and attitudes then.

Whatever had kept me out of this particular church, which was only a block or two from my apartment, I felt myself one evening drawn to the door of the library, to look at the window display of books and pamphlets, and then go in. A priest was alone there, reading behind a desk, and he looked up as I entered. He was a big man, husky, his chest and shoulders straining under his tight black clerical suit coat. A blond man, he had, I saw in a moment, amazingly light blue eyes, eyes that had what I can only call a mild, demure look that wasn't effeminate.

St. Ignatius was a Jesuit church, I learned later, so he must have been one, though that would have meant very little to me at the time. After he asked me in a rather high-pitched voice if he could help me, I told him, jumping right into it to my surprise, that I was "interested" in Catholicism but was far from being able to make any move toward the Church, and he said that there was perhaps some help he could in fact give. We sat facing each other across the little desk. I described my background in a few words, told him about my experience with the Gilson book (which he didn't comment on), and, as I warmed up, finding myself getting almost eloquent, threw over to him the psychological difficulties I had with the idea of being a Catholic, and even tossed him my revulsion from the way the Church existed intellectually and physically now.

He would nod, smile from time to time as though in recognition and even, it seemed to me, occasional confirmation of what I was saying, and ask a question now and then, most often about what I had read in religion and particularly in Catholicism. Throughout our conversation, which lasted more than an hour, during which time two or three middle-aged and one younger woman, all of whom appeared to be regulars, came in and he quickly and cheerfully attended to them, I kept thinking that there was something much too simple about him, almost simpleminded, although I didn't get this impression from anything he specifically said. He seemed in fact to be at least superficially acquainted with the names of the writers and thinkers I kept throwing out and with the "advanced" ideas I brought up.

I mention this because all the time I was with him I kept struggling against a strong feeling of what in all honesty I

Intellectualism

have to call contempt, not for him directly but for his, and the library's, representative status as purveyors of Catholic intellectuality, which I still considered a contradiction in terms. Indeed, when every so often I would glance at some of the nearby shelves and racks, I could see titles exemplary of that thick saccharine piety which I had seen as coating all the churches I had visited.

And so I sat there with complicated emotions, wondering why I was there yet feeling strangely at peace, until I finally decided it was time to leave. By then the priest had partly won me over, though I'm fairly sure he wasn't trying to. He radiated a quality I later understood as serenity and even interpreted as such at moments when I was with him. But at other times I saw it as a kind of gross innocence, a naive acceptance that reached out to embrace everything and everyone indiscriminately; he must never have had, I remember thinking, any doubts about anything whatsoever.

I don't mean I thought him cocksure in his faith, nothing like that. But I could imagine him calmly and trustfully handing over whatever happened in his life, good or bad, satisfying or distressing, to God or the Holy Ghost (as the term was then; now it's the Holy Spirit) or the operation of Grace, all of which were abstractions to me. I could imagine him handing *me* and my situation over as soon as I left, if he hadn't already done so.

He had extremely unsophisticated literary and cultural tastes but he didn't try to press his opinions on me and didn't quarrel with mine. Before I left he had me fill out an application and gave me a card for the library. Then he went to another part of the room which, I later surmised, must have contained books of a "higher" caliber. I went home with several books, a mixed bag: something by G. K. Chesterton, perhaps *The Everlasting Man*, C. S. Lewis's *Miracles* (which surprised me because Lewis was of course a

Protestant) and, what turned out to be most important, a novel by Graham Greene, *The Power and the Glory*, and one by François Mauriac, I forget which one.

I don't think Father Walsh (William Walsh, S.J., the "S.J." striking me as being rather like M.D. or CPA) wholly approved of Greene and Mauriac but he picked out those books with the same alacrity as he had the others. When he gave them to me he said something to the effect of, "There are people who think these novels are very good, though I'm not really qualified to say."

Remembering him, I pause for a moment to honor what he did, for it was a very bold thing. He had seen that I could never have been reached by conventionally pious Catholic literature of the sort he mainly dispensed; he knew that such writing, to the extent that I'd exposed myself to it, had in fact violently increased my doubts about the Church's disposition toward intellect and imagination. I might have told him, or more likely he intuited it, that I needed something much harder, riskier, if I was to overcome my paralysis. So even though he accompanied the whole transaction with a mild warning about problematic theology and disturbing "pessimism," he readily gave me the books that were to prove decisive in the turning of my abstract conversion into a living one.

In a review of one of Mauriac's novels some years ago, Jean Paul Sartre wrote: "God is not a novelist. Neither is M. Mauriac." Sartre objected to the way he thought Mauriac curtailed his characters' freedom, confining them in the claustral atmosphere of a faith that dictated their choices, and this, or some variation of it, has been the traditional criticism of religious novels, in particular Catholic ones. When George Orwell wrote that "the novel is a Protestant art form, requiring the free play of mind. There are few Catholic novelists who are any good, and most of them are bad Catholics," he was surely using "Protestant" in its historical or secular sense, not in its aspect as an active type of faith; from his own position of radical secularism he was really indicting any novelistic stance of belief, however beleaguered, in transcendence and deity.

The great irony surrounding Mauriac is that for most of his career he was subjected to attack from an opposing side; orthodox Catholic commentators found him dangerous because of his "secret sympathy [and] connivance with sin," as one such critic wrote. Beyond that he had to deal with the charge Orwell made: to the extent that he was a good novelist he would have to have been a bad Catholic. André Gide wrote in this vein in his journal in 1931: "If Mauriac had been a more perfect Christian he would not have had subject matter for his books," and he wrote to Mauriac himself once that "the object of your novels is not so much to bring sinners to Christianity as to remind Christians that there is something on earth besides heaven ... Doubtless if I were more of a Christian I would be less your disciple."

It was no good Mauriac's protesting that Gide had him wrong, that he was both a faithful Catholic and an honest novelist, or that, as he wrote in his *Mémoires Intérieures*, he believed "the religious life does not curb, rather does it satisfy the poetic craving ..." He would always be under suspicion, not least because he wrote, with considerable arrogance, in the same book: "Nothing is stranger to the moderns, nothing more distasteful to them when they come across it in its last, Christian possessors, than the metaphysical knowledge of evil."

Well, as I write these pages I'm aware of the antiquated sound the words have. The argument that to be truly religious is to be disqualified from the authentic practice of fiction (and the counterargument that to be religious is to be especially well fitted for it) has lost its force and pertinence in the light of the drastic decline and near disappearance of any fiction that deals with human experience in a context of formal belief or, at least as often, of belief under siege. Who writes such books anymore and who still reads, with any sympathetic interest in their doctrinal or creedal implications, the earlier novels of this kind?

The religious or spiritual novel is in some sense only a memory, but it is just this memory that takes possession of me now, at this stage in my chronicle. There was a time when for me, and for many others, religious fiction, insofar as it was literature and not evangelism or covert apologetics, was as genuine as any other, beset with particular difficulties, to be sure, but not made illegitimate by its subject or motive. Sartre, I've always thought, was only half right: God isn't a novelist but François Mauriac certainly was.

At the time I took home the novels Father Walsh had given me I had long since surrendered myself to the large, general world of fiction and at this period loved certain writers extravagantly: Dostoevsky, Flaubert, Mann, Kafka, Proust most of all. I'd learned in high school, as we all had, that the novel had been given its name because it brought "news," behavioral, emotional, moral and spiritual information people couldn't obtain elsewhere, and I'd learned too that at one time the novel was in its most serious aspect chiefly considered a guide to life or, the other side of the matter, a cautionary account of the way things could go wrong.

But at the time I'm writing of I had no notion that there could be such a thing as a religious novelist, most especially a Catholic one, or that, if there were, he or she could be anything but an apologist, an imagination under orders. Moreover I knew that in one of its modes fiction was (as it chiefly remains) a flight from the responsibilities of perception, the invention of a vulgar kind of alternative world in which what is "seen" is what has previously been desired and desired precisely in order to evade the claims of the actual. Escapist fiction is that which substitutes for experience instead of interrogating it or revealing it in a new light, and I thought that religious fiction, insofar as I thought about it at all, was just such a substitute, as indeed up to the Night of the Book I thought religion itself was.

When I got home from the lending library I read *Miracles*, a short book, before I went to sleep. I remember being more impressed with its logic and charm than I think I would be now. The next day I picked up the Greene novel. I'd read things of his before, some of his thrillers and "entertainments," which I'd quite liked, but *The Power and the Glory* was the first "serious" book of his I'd read. When I finished it a day or two later I remember telling myself that it was the first contemporary novel I had read that dealt with the idea of sin, with human weakness at a level deeper than the psyche or ordinary morality. It was the first fiction of our time that I knew of in which something you could call the soul—not the "heart" or the psyche—confronted the body. In *The Power and the Glory* this confrontation was between the battered, strung-out soul of the whiskey priest, desperately clinging to some point of attachment in transcendence, and his abased, fearful body.

Later as Father Walsh fed me more books on subsequent visits and as I went looking for things on my own, I read much more of Greene and Mauriac, came upon Georges Bernanos and discovered his and Mauriac's predecessors, Léon Bloy, Péguy and Claudel, all figures of what I learned was called in France the "Catholic Revival," composed of writers whose inspiration and subject was radical Catholic experience. (It only occurs to me now that apart from Greene all the writers who were to be so instrumental in my moving to the Church were French and that this was consistent with my having loved French literature more than any other before this.)

I suppose that on the simplest level, but one full of surprise to me, what I got from these writers was a recognition that Catholics, living ones or not long dead, could in fact be writers, literary artists. Before this the only ones I could think of from all history were Dante and the English Jesuit poet Gerard Manley Hopkins. Once I assimilated this I gained from these books the awareness of another realm than I had been accustomed to in literature, and that seemed especially close to some of my circumstances. I spoke of sin a moment ago, and what did I mean? I didn't mean crime or wrongdoing or immorality as those things are generally understood within the ordinary secular world. Sin has something to do with an absolute, with the refusal of some fundamental imperative and therefore of some primary connection.

Crime and Punishment, the book to which I kept comparing the novels I was reading now, ought really to have been called *Sin and Punishment*, as it is in Russian, where the word we translate as "crime" signifies that but also "transgression." Remember how after his murder of the old woman Raskolnikov steps outside and almost instantly feels himself to be in a frozen world, an endless ice-steppe the moral universe has been changed into. The murder has cut him off, from his fellowmen to be sure, but also from something deeper, a source or absolute, and his punishment, satisfactory enough within the human, societal realm, has also to be an expiation, a spiritual process beyond society's claims or understanding.

Salvation and damnation: these terms, up to this time entirely abstract to me yet also, in my dogged secularity, repugnant, took on a dramatic quality in the novels I was reading; they seemed to be worth fighting about, worth imagining. Henry James once said of Ibsen that his plays were about "thinkable things," and that wonderful phrase describes what the novels I was reading were about too.

In relation to all this were the questions of love, passion and desire. In these books desire of various kinds, but sexual desire mostly, was connected to sin with infinitely greater subtlety and compassion than anything my previous notions of Catholicism, or of religion in general, had found room for. I had been repelled by the Church in part because of my conviction that Catholicism existed now largely as a bulwark against lust, which is to say sexual immorality conceived of in the widest manner; it seemed to have no place for love on a human, and so necessarily problematic, ground.

In the writers I was reading, for all their differences of temperament, depth and quality of belief, and so on, and for all their varying mise-en-scènes, I saw that love and desire could be in a sort of reciprocity with sin, that they could have a strange dependence on one another. (This of course is just what Mauriac's Catholic detractors found so dangerous an idea in him.) Sex in these books was perilously involved with spiritual hurt and possible loss, and earthly desire was unendingly pitted against the hope of Heaven. But I saw that one didn't have to choose between the flesh and spirit; one could choose to live, one couldn't help living, in the anguished fertile tension in which body and soul are held.

Of all the novels I read during those weeks the most affecting and important to me were Bernanos's *Diary of a Country Priest*, Mauriac's *The Desert of Love* and *Vipers' Tangle* and Greene's *The Heart of the Matter* and *The End of the Affair*. I've read them all again recently. The Bernanos, that grave, lovely tale of the dying young curate, afflicted with a "deep, inexplicable incompetence, [a] supernatural clumsiness," who is devoted to God yet anguished by his impending loss of the world's beauty, is the only one of them that isn't concerned in some way with sexual desire and, though I don't think it's for that reason, the one that holds up most firmly as literary art.

I'm still touched by the others and continue to respect them, but I see their defects as I didn't then: Mauriac's occasional arbitrary endings and rhetorical questioning—"Of what use is a virtuous existence? What way of escape can it provide? What power has God over passion?"; Greene's occasional contrivances, especially the unconvincing miracles in the last part of *The End of the Affair*, and the tic in his work of pat little melancholy wisdom, too many lines like "He felt the loyalty we all feel to unhappiness—the sense that that is where we really belong."

But I didn't see the flaws then and, what's more, I didn't respond then most strongly, as I do now, to the purely human aspects of the tales (if I can make such a separation), the sweet, beleaguered, doomed loves. The first time I read these novels what took hold of me was the theme of human love, caught in the trap of religious belief, the idea of sexual hunger in fierce relation to the transcendent, the struggle between erotic desire and the imperious purity of the supernatural. Whereas now, in my nearly total state of unbelief, the religious elements strike me as somewhat forced, in a peculiar way almost irrelevant. Such a criticism might seem to invalidate my claim of literary stature for these novelists, as *Catholic* writers, but I don't think so; it's more that I've changed, that the "news" I look for now is of another order.

I wanted to hear about God then, an abstraction at the time, as he has become again. And he was there, lurking in all these fictional worlds, more or less a factor in the plots, often an antagonist, and his presence there—*His* presence; I suddenly remember the usage of faith and even of journal-

God is not real — not merely the Truth

ism—had the effect of making him—Him!—more human, if I can put it in that bizarre way. Certainly it made Him more distinctive. He could fit into literature, I thought, He wasn't just a value, even the Supreme one, He wasn't merely sublimity or the Good or the Truth or the Way, none of which was of any use to me at the time. He was *someone*, a character not wholly unlike all the others.

As I think back on it the most significant thing I gained from these novels was a sense of the pain of being a Catholic, of the losses becoming one would surely entail. The value of this was that it counteracted the bland assurances of inner peace and harmony which were the central elements of the Catholic evangelism I'd previously encountered here and there (one source was the pamphlets I'd occasionally take from racks in the anterooms of churches) and couldn't begin to trust, no matter how much I might have wished to.

But I could trust these writers because I relied on the truths of literature generally. If I were to become a Catholic, they seemed to be telling me, it would be painful in certain ways, it would mean new dilemmas and new kinds of anguish, and this was far more believable than anything I'd heard before in the Church's promises and seductions. Gilson hadn't promised anything, and from where else would I get reliable information? For how can any aggressive or simply self-assured institutional religion advertise the defeats and losses that adhering to it would entail? It was up to those on the margins, the embattled ones, the voices of despair in a dialogue with faith, to tell me the *unofficial* story, which, in any sphere, is always the truer one.

One more point. When I was preparing to write this section I discovered some etymological facts I should have known long ago: that the word "narrative" comes from the Latin for "to tell" and the word "tale" is from the Anglo-

Saxon or Middle English "talu," one of whose chief meanings is "speech."

I looked up those words because I wanted to confirm if I could my suspicion that the peculiarly intense quality of attestation, of bearing witness, that I'd found in those novels long ago, was an aesthetic matter as much as a religious one and that in fact their being works of literary art was just what gave them their credibility as spiritual testimony. I wanted to yoke this fiction as securely as I could to the oldest tradition. And so as I started to write these last pages I had this to work with: narratives, tales, have always been matters of speaking, telling; they imply voices and voices with religious cadences, such as the ones I listened to years ago, as believably—or not—as any other.

A few weeks after I met Father Walsh I decided to invite him to dinner at our apartment. I had told my wife about him and she, in the precariousness of the connections that remained between us, was open to anything that might add a new factor to our stymied situation.

It was a warm summer evening. When the priest arrived he brought into the room his bulky physique along with that strange quality of luminous shyness that had struck and partly discomfited me from the beginning. Throughout the evening he seemed neither greatly ill at ease nor fully at home; he wasn't jocular (he never was) though he wasn't grim either. He was "elsewhere," as in part I'd always known him to be, but he carried this other ambiance into our presence as if to say, "If my being here can do you some good, show you some possibility or other, then that's why I've come."

Yet as the evening went on I noticed in him a touch of what I have to call embarrassment. It showed itself in the way his astonishing blue eyes would focus periodically on a spot on the wall above our heads and in how he sat, not stiffly but as though provisionally, all the time he was with us. It showed too in something less easily definable: a slight strain in communicating, in choosing words, the kind of thing that colors any meeting between people of different cultures or backgrounds who can't be sure they're being understood. It affected us too.

I had invited a friend, a very intelligent woman who had shown some interest in religion. We had drinks, made small talk about the neighborhood and similar matters and then sat down to dinner. I remember that every once in a while I would have a sudden sense of the incongruity, the oddness of this man in a clerical collar sitting in my living room. I remember thinking how more than odd it would have seemed to my parents and even more my grandparents, though this didn't trouble me; if anything, I probably took a measure of pride in being so much more "liberated" than they had been.

It was our friend Luna Tarlo who now took the conversation toward spiritual matters as the meal went on. I can't remember much of what we specifically talked about, only that the priest offered neither dogmas nor "answers" of any great weight. Not that we asked him profound questions. Mostly we discussed certain Catholic practices that puzzled us, such as Confession or the Mass, or the meaning of notions like "papal infallibility" or the Immaculate Conception.

The only time I noticed any real tightness in him, a drawing back as though from a subject that wasn't quite discussable, wasn't really within his sense of the appropriate, was when the conversation touched, extremely lightly, on sexual matters, more specifically on the Church's position on birth control or priestly celibacy. Within the tightness he handled these topics reasonably enough, and for the rest he gave off an air of assurance, with nothing condescending in it, about the value and possible consequence to us of the rough, stumbling, partly naive inquiries we were making.

I found reinforced an impression I had had before: that he would never try to move or urge me to any step, that he'd never preach. It wasn't a strategy on his part, I felt sure. Perhaps it was simply an aspect of his nature, his shyness, for example. Yet as the evening went on I felt more and more sure that this restraint was an action of love, disinterested love, to be sure, yet responsible: it took me into account. I couldn't return love to him, or even affection; he was too alien to me, too far outside the categories I'd created for the people I met. But I felt myself in a strange, both intimate and remote, relation with him, that was evident.

After he left, with a little wave, a shy thank you and a sort of backing of his big body through the doorway, the three of us talked about him for a while, agreeing that we'd never met anyone like him. We didn't quite trust his goodness, we all said, and were a bit ashamed of that, but, we all said too, he certainly did run counter to the image of a Catholic priest we had had. Then I walked with our friend to her apartment a couple of blocks away. We talked about Father Walsh some more, Luna saying at one point that despite all the doubts she still had, she'd felt peculiarly "better" in his presence, to which I replied that I had too. Then I left her at her door and began to walk back home.

I was still thinking about the evening—the question of feeling "better" was in my mind; it seemed somehow sloppy, sentimental, but it had been real—when after I'd walked a little way I stopped for a red light at the corner of Seventy-ninth and Third. It turned to green. I stepped from the curb and started to cross the street and at that moment, in a rush of light-headedness and with the same sensation of having been taken over that I had felt in connection with the

Gilson book in the library, I began to say out loud in a low voice that was at the same time excited and tearful, almost heartbroken, the words of the Hail Mary, words of a prayer I hadn't known before but which came now as though I'd been repeating them all my life: "Hail Mary, full of grace! the Lord is with thee, blessed art thou among women, and blessed is the fruit of thy womb, Jesus," and the rest. (I remember the word "womb" seeming strange to me, slightly unpleasant, but slipping out as easily as the others.) Before I reached my door I must have said the complete prayer a dozen times, in the same broken and astonished voice.

Whatever explanation there might have been for this eerie event I couldn't find it in any rational place. I had never heard the Hail Mary, had never read it; I'm pretty sure I didn't even know what it was.

My sojourns in churches had never taken place during any activities of worship, and I had made it a point to sit as far as I could from anyone else in the church, anyone who might have been murmuring the prayer, as someone once suggested to me could have happened. Nor had I heard it in the street or over the radio. A "learn-while-you-sleep" cassette under my pillow? I'm pretty sure they didn't exist in those days, but even if they'd been around who could have fashioned the tape on this one and then have sneaked into my bedroom on such a bizarre evangelical mission?

And even if against all likelihood I did have the prayer buried somewhere in my unconscious, what had made it leap to my tongue at that moment and in that way, with such mingled sorrow and ardor, and what compelled me to go on repeating it with an obstinate tenacity that was made up partly of fear of letting it go and partly of gratitude for its being there? For all during the four or five minutes I walked along intoning those words of the prayer I was afraid, in the midst of my bewilderment and tears, that the compulsion might suddenly disappear and, even more, that the whole episode would in fact turn out to be explicable on rational grounds, that it would turn out to be in the realm of the psychological, instead of the swift, fatal visit from the supernatural I wanted it, this time, to be.

The gratitude I spoke of wasn't directly to Father Walsh, with whom I couldn't help but connect the occurrence, or to the Virgin Mary, whom I had scarcely ever thought of and didn't much like whenever I did happen to think of her, and whose name I kept repeating now without conscious belief or any picture of her in my head except perhaps for a vague, sentimental holy card sort of image I snuffed out as soon as the experience was over. No, the gratefulness I felt was offered to whatever existed that could plunge so imperiously into my frozen soul and mind, although this unknown force or being couldn't yet have for me the name of God.

A few weeks have gone by. I've been reading much of the time and saying the Hail Mary several times a day, neither fervently nor perfunctorily but as though it simply were a new useful habit I'd picked up. Or more likely I kept saying it out of a superstitious fear that if I stopped, something else that had been set in motion would also stop.

I haven't gone to see Father Walsh, toward whom I now feel a strange, or perhaps not so strange, embarrassment. In thinking about this I decide that the reason I don't want to tell him about the incident (I haven't told anybody) is that it's propelled me further along toward what has begun to seem an inevitable destination but one I still find alarming, incredible; I don't want to have to tell him that.

Still, I'm no longer fighting the process the way I had. I've taken to going into Father Walsh's church, St. Ignatius Loyola, the one around the corner from me on Park Avenue. Mostly I sit there looking on from the back pews during an early Mass. At those times, though, I'm still half poised for flight.

And now on a gray misty afternoon in late winter or early spring of 1953 I find myself standing outside another little lending library, whose name and auspices I forget, though I do remember that it was on East Seventy-second Street. I start to move on and then something makes me walk in, no real urgency but a definite impulse. So I go through the door, look around and begin to browse. The place seems empty except for the gray-haired librarian, who glances up at me from behind her desk and then goes back to whatever she's been doing. And then I catch sight of a woman standing in a corner and reading a book. I move to a position where I can look at her unobserved, for I've been immediately, helplessly struck by her.

I can see that she's very beautiful, or once was, or still is but has put herself under wraps. She's maybe forty or at most forty-five, with slightly graying black hair cut without any style (was it in a bun? I can't remember). She isn't wearing any makeup, which in those days indicated a particularly aggressive "naturalness" in a woman or else an extreme indifference to appearance, and she's dressed frumpily in a boxy coat, thick black stockings and clumsy shoes. But she has a marvelously clear, pure profile, which reminds me of some Renaissance head, a della Robbia or Piero della Francesca, and when she looks up briefly I see that she has very dark, deep-set eyes.

I watch her from the corner of my eye for a few minutes while pretending to be studying a book I've picked out. Then I find myself edging over to where she's standing. She's in front of what I can now see is a section of books on religion and I immediately think, dammit, not again! Then she turns at my approach, looks directly at me and says, astonishingly, "I think you'll be interested in this," at the same

86

time holding out to me the book she's been reading. I have all I can do to keep from dropping to the floor in a heap. In the instant before I take the book from her outstretched hand I have time to think: what is this conspiracy of books that's taking charge of my life, arranging my conversion, if that's what it's to be; who's issuing me this library card for salvation?

I ended up with the book she had offered me but I can't remember what it was or whether I read it later, though I know I must have. What I recall next is our sitting across from each other having coffee in a nearby luncheonette (nostalgic word!) while she explained, if that could possibly be the right term, why she'd done what she had. She told me that she had noticed me several times in St. Ignatius, where she went every morning to early Mass, and that I had seemed to her, she didn't at first say why, to be in need of help.

"You didn't seem desperate," she said with a smile, "but more like restless and uneasy. Maybe it was the way you kept looking around. Anyway I was sure you weren't a Catholic and I thought . . . Well I decided the other day that the next time I saw you in church I was going to speak to you, and then you came up to me in the library a little while ago."

Naturally I couldn't tell her that I had gone over to her out of nothing like the motive she had had in deciding to approach me. I had been attracted to her physically, it was as simple as that, I thought. And as we talked, the attraction grew and did it in the face of everything she was saying. For the thing she had really divined (an apt word, as it turned out) was the truth: that I was in a state of siege. I felt more and more drawn to conversion, or rather I had begun to think it inevitable but was still unable to cooperate with the plan.

87

She could only try to explain how she knew this by telling me that because of her own history and present spiritual situation she had a peculiar alertness and receptivity to anyone whose bearings, or inner condition, might have affinities or potential ones to hers. In my case, she said, she had a strong impulse to help.

I don't remember more than a fraction of what we said that afternoon, for our conversations were to go on for many weeks and to merge with one another in my memory. In the end they made up the deepest, most detailed self-revelation I'd ever given to anyone, and I know that I began by offering the roughest summary of my background and present state of mind. As we went on in our "friendship" I told her more about the recent spiritual events or "miracles" and the turbulence they had brought, and gave her some details of my sexual longings and confusions, putting much more emphasis, however, on that side of my erotic nature which could be thought of as more or less normal; this was the side from which I was in fact continually pressing toward her.

In return she told me some basic facts about herself, though I couldn't help thinking that they were somewhat edited. A "secular nun" is the description I'd give of her now, even though she used nothing like those words at the time, nor did it occur to me to use them.

She had been an actress, she told me, a very promising one with a career well under way. (I had never heard of her but, then, I wasn't much interested in the theater in those days so I didn't have any reason to disbelieve her.) Something over ten years ago she had suddenly been "stricken" (her word) with a simultaneous revulsion from the life of the theater, with its clamor of egos and its sexual fevers, and a "hunger" for God, which was the terse way she described it.

She had been born a Catholic (she was Irish), had believed without questioning anything she was taught and followed every precept and practice, and then had gradually abandoned the Faith in her late teens and had lived thereafter as an impregnable unbeliever. She had gotten married in her early twenties and been divorced a few years later; she told me nothing about her husband. After the initial burst of desire her movement back to the Church had been a slow, slipping and sliding, often painful process. Once back inside, she said, she had been entirely chaste, as well as wholly without material or worldly desires. (She didn't use those words; their pomposity is my own doing, but I've decided to let them stand.)

She had lived for some years, she told me, in a basement room in a large Park Avenue apartment house. When I first saw it I was shocked by how small it was, tiny and windowless, with a ceiling so low my hair almost touched it. Every morning she would go to the earliest Mass at St. Ignatius down the street and then on weekdays to some sort of office job about which she gave no details.

In the evenings and on weekends she would read, mostly religious books of a mystical or nontechnical theological kind, and poetry, listen to music on a cheap record-player someone had given her, pray and take walks in Central Park.

I don't remember whether she told me all this that first day or if I picked up the information bit by bit as we went along. What I also don't remember, and am pretty sure didn't happen, was any moment when I had doubts about any part of her story. Had I met her even a few months earlier (hardly likely!) I surely would have regarded her with the ordinary skepticism of the ordinary rationalist; more than that, I know I would have seen her as a melancholy, even pathological instance of defeat, a "loser," had that term been in use at the time. As it was, I took in her story with a kind of avidity, seeing its strangeness as a mystery to be esteemed. And I fell for her in every sense, swept away from the moment I saw her.

Very quickly a pattern set into our meetings, almost a ritual. We would come together nearly every morning at early Mass, sitting or kneeling side by side in a rear pew; I was the tourist still and she was the cicerone who was there to point out and explain things. Then we'd meet again for coffee in the afternoon. One or two evenings a week I would come to her room and we would talk, about the day or about ourselves, most often about religion, belief and practice. She never asked me about my wife, although I had told her I was married. She kept a bottle of Scotch for me—she never drank—and would wave away my offers to pay for it or bring my own.

Then there was a bench in Central Park near the Metropolitan Museum where we would often meet late in the afternoon at a prearranged time if for any reason we had missed each other earlier in the day, and sometimes because we knew in the morning that we couldn't have gone through the rest of the day apart. We would take walks, strolling arm in arm or hand in hand or with our arms round one another's waist, like lovers, though if that was what we were it was an exceedingly odd kind of amour.

For from the beginning she calmly and agilely deflected the movements of physical desire I made, a desire that was at the very center of the swiftly growing emotion I felt. She didn't want passion, she told me more than once, except for God; she didn't want me to love her except in Him. She would teach me about Him, she said, show me how to overcome my doubts and fears. She would lead me to the Church, where she assured me I would find grace and strength, and then she would step out of my life.

For a long time I fought both madly and, I thought, cunningly against her quiet self-containment, the loftiness of her attitude, the serene way, for example, she would forestall my attempts to embrace her with passion, scenes that would usually end with her kissing me softly on the forehead. I felt more and more like a character in a Greene novel (and sometimes like one in a farce), caught between two demands, two dimensions of being, and it took me a long time to surrender to one of them, if I ever really did.

For without ever doubting the depth and ardor of her spirituality and without failing to be amazed by her austere self-possession, I was never quite sure that she wasn't in part deluding herself about her feelings for me, and this doubt encouraged me to make repeated attempts to make love to her. For how else could I account for the way her hand kept squeezing and exploring mine as we walked, or the way her eyes would light up whenever she saw me coming toward her?

And what was I to make of the letters and notes she wrote me, sometimes mailing them but more often leaving them (rashly it might seem) in the foyer of my building, inserting them in books she lent me, leaving them with the waitress in the coffee shop we went to, and once or twice scotch-taping them to the underside of the bench in the park we'd made our own (I would feel under the seat with one hand while my other held a book or newspaper I pretended to be reading: a spy, a Russian agent!) when for some reason she wasn't going to be able to meet me. It was an astonishing outpouring of communications, sometimes as many as three or four a day.

There would be long letters—missives it would be more accurate to call them—filled with religious musings and spiritual advice or quotes from things she'd been reading or comments on my own letters to her or on things I had said. Once she took a rambling, murky letter of mine about my spiritual condition and annotated it with quotes from the Gospels, as if to throw light I couldn't myself find. At the other extreme there would be notes with only one or two sentences, or some cryptic, runish phrase, or a short poem or some lines by Hopkins or Emily Dickinson or Rilke, with no comment.

But what was most disturbing to me were the "love letters" she so often wrote, when, for whatever reason, we'd missed each other in church or hadn't met for a day or two because, as happened once or twice, she had been sick or I had been or, as also happened a couple of times, we'd quarreled about something. These letters sent my blood leaping. They were filled with lines like these: "I thought I would die when you didn't come to Mass this morning"; "I looked for you like I was looking for the other half of my soul"; "You cannot imagine how much you are loved."

I've summoned these words from memory, but now memory takes a jump and I rush to my files, for it comes to me that I saved some of her letters. I haven't seen them in many years and it takes me a good while before I dig them out, a little packet with a rubber band around it. Ruth. I read over your letters to me and am swept with pain and, yes, longing.

I decide to quote from one letter, to show the reader more eloquently than my own words have done what you were like, Ruth. We'd had an argument about Scobie in Greene's *Heart of the Matter*. And you wrote to me:

> You see, when you began to talk about Scobie's suicide with such sympathy, I went blind for a moment because I was only thinking about the fact that you had begun in prayer, and knowing that there are desolations in that way I suddenly feared that you were becoming enamored of the idea of hurting yourself in this way ... it is not unheard of, you know, and I became fierce. Like a tiger over her cub. I wouldn't become fierce over an idea. Not with

you. May He forgive me for becoming fierce over anything when I am in your presence. But see how you help
me. With you I can learn how to stop being uncouth. You
always give me some little gifts like this when I see you. I
believe that you will always believe in me. I trust you.
You are not only a dear child, but even a man—and can
bear things.

Then you went on, Ruth, to attack Scobie's presumption:
"who is [he] to flout God in the name of charity?" And then
you told me that you "felt a little tormented" at having argued with me again. And you ended: "But at noon I went
out and had something to eat, and then took a brisk walk
about. Everything became lighter, and I was running all
around the park looking for a leper to kiss. How I love you,
Richard."

I tried to read letters like this as though their tropes and
images were of the same order as that of certain religious
poets I'd been reading, largely at her instigation. Saint John
of the Cross and Saint Teresa of Ávila had employed a vocabulary of secular, physical, quasi-erotic love as a stammer-
ing, inadequate means of expressing their passion for the
divinity. But I never quite succeeded in these exegeses, if for
no other reason than that read in this way the letters equated
me with the divine. To the end a letter of this kind would
instantly make me dizzy with desire and confusion, and to
very near the end I held on to a hope that somehow I'd find a
way to vault over or slip underneath her spirit to reach her
body.

It's true that there were times when I found her nearly
impossible to be with, so impermeable was her serenity and
so otherworldly her chief manner. At such times she dwindled for me to a point of light or, worse, she evanesced into a
principle, a combination of admonishment and succor; by
contrast, I would find myself feeling gross, all too fleshly.

But then something would happen to restore her to me, some mutual recognition or shared wit, and I would recover my ardor. I remember once dissolving with delight when as we sat on our park bench she suddenly said, "There are so many people in the world," and then, pointing to some passersby, "There go two more."

The end. It came differently from the way she'd predicted, for it was I who brought it about. Nothing I've written so far better exemplifies the traps and corruptions of memory. As I was planning this section and even in my first draft of the entire book I remembered Ruth as having left *me*; I saw her as having suddenly dropped out of my life, as she had said she someday would; I even wrote about my frantic search for her, her not being home or not answering the door, and of my gradual acceptance of my loss.

But it didn't happen that way. Among the packet of her letters and notes to me I found this one: "Gone forever? Temporarily lost? Wounded? Detached? Sick? In trouble? Try once more. 555." (In accordance with our little spy fantasy—the bench in the park—we had given each other secret numbers; I can't remember mine.)

Now it all came back to me: I had left her. What had happened was that in a moment of bravado, perhaps, or from a rush of desire to please her, or maybe out of desperation, I had told her that despite my fears I thought I was ready for the Church. She had agreed and had arranged for me to talk to a priest she knew, a man, she said, notable for his kindness and understanding. And I had copped out. I'd fled, from her, from the priest (I didn't call him), from the terrifying direction my life had been taking.

More than once in the following weeks and months I became almost sick with longing for her. But I stayed away from St. Ignatius, the park, the coffee shop and any other place I might have been likely to run into her. I tried, too, to repudiate the idea of Catholicism, of becoming one, but it hung on; just below the surface it rested, recovering from this temporary setback.

Remembering Ruth now, I know that she had brought me a long way toward the Church, too far, perhaps, considering my readiness at that time. She had done it through argument, patient explanation and, most effectively, through her own example of calm trust. She had taught me practical things, such as how to make the sign of the cross, how to read a missal and what the various stages of the Mass meant, so that I would know what to do during the ceremony. She had convinced me that Confession, about whose efficacy I had had serious doubts, was indeed a powerful sacrament (she had even taught me what that word meant) and that a practice like fasting during Lent was something dignified and worthwhile.

She had also taught me to pray. I don't mean she told me what prayers to say at various times, although there was a little of that, too, but how to get into the right frame of mind and what bodily positions one might assume, which to my surprise was a more flexible matter than just being on your knees or standing with your head bowed. I still had great difficulty getting prayers out, the only one that came easily being the Hail Mary, but she told me that you could *think* a prayer even when you couldn't say the words aloud. And, most subtly, she taught me what faith meant, and hope: they were practical virtues, daily assistances, not modes of dreaming.

It took time but I gradually became reconciled to . . . having *lost* her, I was about to write, but it was really to having thrown her away, and began to resume my stumbling movement toward the Church. I had been closer in ways to this woman than I had ever been to anyone, and yet there had been that distance which made it seem at times that we were on different planets. She had rescued me from loneliness and had flattered and encouraged me, too, by her passionate attachment and care for me, however concerned that was, I might wryly reflect, for my welfare in eternity, and more directly by reading my little writings and making wonderfully perceptive if largely unschooled comments on them, at the same time caressing me with praise. When I left her, in my terror, everything was in place for what I would eventually do—or become.

A few months later my wife and I separated and I got into our car—a Kaiser, of all long-dead makes!—and drove out west. I was heading for Colorado Springs, where a friend of mine, a man I had met when we were both in the Marines overseas, was the assistant curator of an art museum. I drove for two days and nights and another day, catching a few hours of sleep once in a cornfield in Kansas or Missouri, and late in the afternoon of the third day rolled into the parking lot of the museum just as my friend was coming out.

I hadn't seen him for several years and hadn't written that I was coming, but in a way that was characteristic of him he dryly and laconically acknowledged my arrival, didn't ask any questions and told me to follow his car to his house for dinner. That evening I told him—Richard, or Dick, Grove—and his wife, Kay, much of my story, including of course the religious interest but leaving out how close I actually was to conversion. I suppose I edited my narrative because I knew they were ardent secular liberals and so wouldn't have been likely to be sympathetic. I think now that I wasn't doing them justice.

The next day he got me a job cataloging American Indian artifacts in the basement of the museum. I didn't know a thing about the subject but with his help and a great many books I managed to do the work, which wasn't at all boring or unpleasant. My pay was forty dollars a week, which at the time wasn't all that bad and was certainly enough for my needs: six dollars a week for the clean, pleasant rooming house where I stayed, a little for cigarettes, gas and incidentals, and something for the contributions I made to the dinners I mostly ate with Kay and Dick.

They were nothing but kind to me, yet most of the time I was there I lived in a state of desperate loneliness, cut off from my past and with the future stretching ahead as limbo. The separation from my wife had been largely at her instigation and was painful, which surely played a part in what happened next. It wasn't that I made the fateful decision to become a Catholic because of the break in my marriage but, then again, perhaps I did do it for that reason, *at that time.* I mean I would have become a Catholic eventually, of that I'm sure, for the process had become irreversible. But I wouldn't have done it that soon ("God, send me chastity . . . but not yet"!) and maybe not until some other upheaval took place in my life, some new knife of disaster slicing away familiar and safe contexts.

A few days after I got to Colorado Springs I began to go to early Mass, usually at six o'clock, in a lovely little Spanish-American church I had come across. It was a simple place, with a clean whitewashed exterior and a minimum of modest decoration inside. My fellow worshipers were almost all old or middle-aged Mexican women, with a sprinkling of old men, and the two priests, both rather young, were Mexican-Americans too, or so I assumed from their appearance.

This went on for a week or two and then one day I rang the doorbell of the rectory attached to a big, reddish-brown, gloomy church I'd been told was the cathedral. A tall blond priest who appeared to be about the same age as I was showed me in. I sat down on a leather chair in a small room and he sat opposite me while I gave him a highly truncated version of my story, finishing by saying that I was eager, "desperate" was the word I think I used, to be baptized. He quizzed me, not at all belligerently, and ended by telling me that even though it was clear to him that I knew much more than was technically necessary I would have to take a course of instruction. Before I left he told me that he too had been born Jewish and had been converted in his late teens, but he didn't give me any details.

For a month or so we met two or three times a week in the evenings or late afternoons discussing religion and going over various Catholic doctrines and procedures. He didn't strike me as particularly intelligent, and in fact I kept having to suppress a dislike for him—there was something priggish in his manner—and I threw away after a glance the uninspiring or actively obnoxious pamphlets he gave me to take home.

I fought off a final attack of fear and doubt. Christmas seemed an appropriate time. And so the evening came which I described at the beginning of the book, and I was ushered in, through a thin stream of water and a Latin formula, to a new way of existence, given a new set of terms with which to describe and consider myself.

Chapter 2

I T WAS TO BE FIVE OR SIX WEEKS AFTER MY BAPTISM BE-
fore I could begin to think of leaving Colorado Springs.
My strongest reason for staying there was that I needed
the anonymity the place afforded, the way it served as a
hideout from my past. Moreover to have gone back to New
York immediately or anytime soon after the event that had
been the most dangerous and original movement of my life
would have been to recklessly expose myself to shock; it
would have been like walking out nude into the snow. As it
was I needed time to "recuperate."

To borrow another metaphor from the realm of the body,
it was as though I had been in an automobile accident in that
western resort town, was recovering from my injuries and
now had to learn to walk in an altered way before I'd be allowed to go home. So I practiced my steps on the hospital
grounds, a peculiar species of convalescent; I was someone
trying to adapt to a new definition of well-being.

The metaphor of illness is scarcely a comfortable one in
regard to conversion experiences, which are almost always
described in terms of regained "health." Yet as I think about
it now it strikes me that the only existential condition that
comes at all close to what I felt mine had been then is that of
illness or physical affliction. I began this chapter with the
image of having been in a hospital after an "accident," the

invisible and healing crack-up that my baptism struck me as being, and of having to learn to walk in a new way. Now I want to extend that idea.

To be sick or disabled is in one of its effects to have been plucked out of the way things usually proceed; ill health is an aberration, slowing you up or bringing you to a standstill. And so to be sick is to be taken out of the race or contest, if one wants to look at it that way, or "left back," the way it can happen to you at school. In any case you have the status and perspective now of a nonparticipant; standing on the sidelines, a certain kind of "failure," you may look on with envy or disgruntlement or self-pity but also, if you take advantage of the stance, you can have a sense of seeing further or deeper than the members of the parade.

Being old, though it most often wraps us in a mist of fearful resignation, can also sharpen our just sense of mortality. Such awareness tends to be suppressed when you're younger, in the midst of active life, swimming in it as in a sustaining ocean, one that becomes boundless, supreme, the totality of what we believe and value. "We were twenty and would never die," Thomas Wolfe had written, and spoke for the powers and buoyancy of the young body, the inadmissibility of an *end*.

The longer people can expect to live, the better life has become in physical ways, the more complex and varied human experience has become—the wider the range of possibilities of every kind—the less has been the need for transcendence, that craning up and away. This is a chief reason why for a long time secularists have thought of religion as a refuge for the old, the weak and the poor. I think of the penniless squatters in De Sica's film *Miracle in Milan* (not an overtly religious work) mounting their broomsticks and soaring above the Duomo toward *somewhere else*, a land "where 'good morning' really means 'good morning.'"

As life improves, or the idea that it may improve gains strength, death recedes, becoming an insult or an aberration, a "misdeed," as Italo Svevo called it; death could always be found hovering behind the desire for transcendence. The present mania for physical prowess, the cult of being "into one's body," has behind it, I think, an unacknowledged widening of the gap between life, *conceived* of as health, and suffering and death, as well as between nature on one side and deity on the other.

I don't want to be misunderstood: to be leery of the multiplicity of joggers and exercise bicycles, the proliferation of health clubs and diets, isn't to believe, perversely, in flabbiness and ill health. But in the vanity of self-absorption, the satisfied contemplation of improved "body tone," I sense the loss of a certain realism, a blindness to mortality. "Health cannot analyze itself even if it looks at itself in the mirror," Svevo wrote in *The Confessions of Zeno*. "It is only we invalids who can know anything about ourselves."

To be sick or very old is to be enabled to see death restored to its sovereignty and so, if you can open yourself to it, to be provisionally sprung free from the pressure to assent exclusively to life, with its obligation to live entirely among the things of this world: God as the visible.

For all these reasons I've more than once thought of my conversion as a kind of illness, if health is to be defined as prowess and delight exclusively within the material, or simply human, social world. And I've thought of it as a kind of death, too, a preparation for the "real" one. One dies to life, previous life; one lives then in a new way.

It wasn't that after my baptism I felt I'd been born again, or, as the term was at that time, reborn. Or if I did feel anything like that it was in a very different sense from what the born-again people tell us they experience. At this stage I just want to point out that Catholicism never served to make me feel justified within this life, nor did I think of it as an agency of self-improvement or, crassest of all, a helping hand to "success." But I didn't think of it as an old people's home or a poorhouse either.

My sense was of living perilously beyond ordinary fate, ordinary choice. Because for someone like me to have become a Catholic hadn't really been a choice at all, at least not within the usual stock of recognizable possibilities. On the one side lay those "natural" fates and dominions, asserting their various claims which I was variously fitted or unfitted to meet, and on the other lay a single claim which seemed to make all the others irrelevant.

I would never have walked over the line or even conceived of doing it on my own. I can't imagine that anyone of my nature and background would have done it on his own. But it seemed to me during those weeks after the baptism that even though I had been *made* to step into a new dimension as the result of having been given some unheard-of kind of help, a push, I'd nevertheless somehow contrived to create myself anew.

So I suppose there was an element of vanity in it. But there was at least as much gratitude, thankfulness for having been picked out, although there were times when it occurred to me that perhaps I'd been chosen just because I'd been so far gone, an extreme case! These two emotions or states of feeling would for a long time make up my prevailing morale about what I had done. Until in time the pressures against *being* a Catholic as opposed to having become one began to mount and I came to feel, with sorrow and great perturbation at first, neither proud nor grateful, finally unable to remember why I had felt both.

There were very few objective changes in the way I lived or what I did during those weeks, with the exception of some physically circumscribed but important matters having to do with Catholic practice. For the most part my life kept to the precise routine I had been following since shortly after I'd come to Colorado, except that now I didn't have to report to the cathedral those two or three times a week for instruction in the Faith.

I was a member of the Faith now and thought of it at the same time as an invisible network of acceptances and obligations and an actual place, the little Mexican-American church I'd been going to before. Every weekday morning I'd get up sometime before six and drive over there in the dark, a journey of ten minutes or so. After Mass I'd have breakfast in a nearby diner and then drive over to the museum for work. Most evenings I would spend at my friends' house talking about books or art or movies and exchanging local gossip, or I'd go to the library of Colorado College, a small nondescript institution, and take books out, mostly philosophy and spiritual works, go home and spend the evening reading or writing long letters to the two or three people in New York or elsewhere with whom I'd been sharing what had been happening to me.

As I remember them now these long, "heartfelt," even passionate outpourings embarrass me. But I don't have to rely on memory. When I recently described this book to a friend who had been one of those correspondents she, Doris Vidiver, came up with a letter I'd written to her, dated New Year's Day, 1954. I quote from that letter now, after overcoming my distaste for the rhetoric and some of the sentiments it displays.

I have done what my whole life for years has been moving toward: I've been baptized and now draw from strength anterior to my own, from unceasing creative, redemptive sources, and from the love which teaches our explorations . . . believe me, dear Doris, it hasn't meant the end of struggle or questioning, nor the defeat of images. It's freed me from what would never let me go—the monster of distrust and disbelief that lay in the interior, feeding on me and sapping me . . . you know me well enough to accept at least the mystery I've entered, because you know that the strength I seek is more than is generally needed, and the aspirations that impel me more beautiful than appetite or even human idealism. I've surrendered, it's true, but to that enemy whose name is friend, to He who gives us the very capacity to refuse to surrender, to the God who permits us to deny Him.

Before I comment on the language of this letter I want to say something about what it reveals of my state of mind, and hence my motives, at the time of my baptism. It isn't unusual for a religious conversion to take place out of a sense of oppression by the self, the weight of it, the way it demands and exhorts and complains; solipsism: "the theory that the self can be aware of nothing but its own experiences and states." My own self had oppressed and alarmed me, and frightened me too; I didn't want to be the only one responsible for it. Hence a "surrender," a handing over of sovereignty.

Then there was the matter of "mystery," which in my case meant I'd moved toward the unknown at least in part because I was weary of the known. I don't mean I was looking for the irrational; Gilson's book had swept me up just because it made belief in God more rational than unbelief was. But the "reasonableness" of faith only meant that it wasn't contrary to logical thinking; beyond that it left space for the unknown, for whatever can't be answered here and now. Mystery, the mystery of faith, is like that of art: what remains after the conscious mind has done its best.

The letter says or implies these things and I'm grateful for its reminders. But as I read over the lines I'm unpleasantly struck by how "elevated" they are, how *literary*. In the way the writing strains toward both lyricism and significance it seems to me to reveal a borrowed quality, an appropriation, no doubt largely unconscious, from some of the more conventionally fervent religious books I'd been reading. More than that, for all its vocabulary of abnegation and surrender it indicates an impulse of self-aggrandizement, the pride I talked about before. I wasn't aware of this when I wrote the letter, or only subliminally, for I thought myself truly humble; I was convinced that my ego had been thoroughly chastened. My education works retroactively as I write.

On Saturday mornings my friend Dick (whom I hadn't told about my having become a Catholic, behind his back so to speak: I never did tell him) and I would go through an almost invariable ritual. We had met through our mutual infatuation with books. On a blasted coral island in the South Pacific called Peleliu I had seen him one day carrying a copy of Dylan Thomas's *New Poems*, which I'd recognized by its purple cover, and he had seen me with, I think, Rilke's *Duino Elegies;* we had circled each other warily for a moment, disbelieving, and had then nearly fallen into one another's arms. Now we would go to the Goodwill and Salvation Army stores and rummage through the used books they had for sale, after having speculated dreamily at breakfast on the wonderful discoveries we were likely to make and on a few occasions actually did. The odd thing was that while I had provisionally given up an active interest in literature in favor of spiritual and philosophical reading I could still get excited by names, titles, the physical book itself. (My God, Dick, look at this! What's *Seven Types of Ambiguity* doing here for a quarter?)

Sundays I would sleep later, to seven or seven-thirty, go

to Mass at eight, have breakfast, go back to my room with the totally inadequate Colorado Sunday papers (the first dim warning I had that I wasn't going to be able to *live* in the Springs even if I wanted to was the way I missed the Sunday *Times*), sift through them, do the simplistic crossword puzzle, and after that take stock of my situation, usually on long solitary walks through the pleasant winterladen town. One road, I remember, was called "Garden of the Gods." Then most often I would go over to the Groves' house for dinner.

As I bring it all to mind I can see now that for all my inner turmoil, those first weeks of my life as a Catholic were dear to me in their intense clarity and effervescent hope. I was lonely and had been uprooted, but there were reasons why in the midst of this I bounded along. Imagine: I was twenty-eight (and looked about nineteen, in splendid physical shape: lean, no waist, heart finely tuned), scarcely encumbered by material responsibilities, and I was starting out. Within the world, the secular one as I had begun to label it, I hadn't any idea at all of what I was starting out for, but that was just the point: I didn't think of myself as for the most part within the secular or "real" world any longer.

The way I had slipped out of it was to have done something I'd have described as extraordinarily "far out," had the term been in use at that time. From my new perspective it seemed to me that very few people ever come close to changing their lives in the radical way I had changed mine (and for all my dislike of the born-again phenomenon I know that the people who describe themselves this way have the same thought). Men and women change their jobs and even careers, get married or divorced, have children, move to new cities or countries, and so on, but their core of self remains essentially the same. For what's been altered are their physical circumstances, their objective situations or even their emotional conditions, but not usually their basic attitudes toward existence nor their judgments about nature, humanity and moral being.

To have a wife or husband (or homosexual lover, for that matter) is a circumstance, just as is the most absorbing career or significant achievement. To be married or not, to be a parent or not, to do this or that kind of work, are all among the types of option most of us are given, in the Western world at least, with richer or thinner components of choice. We come to these possibilities as they await us, or we seek them out; we make decisions (conscious or not, free or heavily influenced; it doesn't affect my point) and then go on within the indicated boundaries. But it seemed to me that what I had done was to step outside the ordinary systems of action and value, and I thought of this with something more like awe than pride.

But of course I was still within the sphere of material necessity, and there my prospects were anything but glittering. I was a cultural stock-clerk making forty dollars a week and the job was due to end soon and wasn't going to lead to anything else. Nor had I any training in anything whatsoever. I wasn't *qualified*. But I didn't worry about this at the time, for my worldly aspirations were very much in abeyance during these weeks, or rather they'd apparently disappeared.

One of the most seductive aspects of a sudden revolution in one's moral and psychic life, such as I'd undergone, is that what has seemed to matter most before matters least now. When material or "natural" ambitions are replaced by transcendent or otherworldly ones you can feel a lightness, a buoyancy, at the same time as you feel the galactic winds from that world of otherness and hear the silence of the invisible domain to which you've risked giving your allegiance. The lightness I felt was in part social—a relief from the stress of having to "develop" myself in relation to everyone else, a relief from competitiveness—and in part emotional and somatic, a lessening of the demands of appetite, gross or delicate as those might be.

It was to turn out in fact that my appetites, like my worldly ambitions, hadn't been expunged at all but were on ice, and when the thaw came they would reassert themselves with growing and finally demoralizing force. But for now all I wanted was to learn how to be what I nominally had become. I wanted, in the rhetoric I used at the time, to progress inwardly, to grow in the spirit, which for the first time I could identify as my soul, something distinct from my psyche though incorporating it. I wanted salvation, not as a verdict but a condition.

Well, you had to work for it, you couldn't have it for the asking. It wasn't simply a matter of believing in Jesus or "accepting" Him into your life (why do most Protestants usually say "Jesus" while Catholics more often say "Christ"? I'll have to find out). Although I was assailed from time to time by attacks of rather dizzying reflection on the enormity of what I'd done, second thoughts one could call them, I felt generally exhilarated and immensely relieved. But there were certain practical considerations, concrete obligations, that rose from my having become a Catholic, my having gone and done it.

My life in the quotidian world, my "civilian" life as I'd come to regard it, went on very much as before. But inside the Church, within those visible and invisible walls, there were many new things I had to do, and together they brought about a turbulence in me that was very complicated, so that I have a hard time sorting it out after all these years.

I was an insider now. When I knelt in church to pray or

went up to the altar rail to take Communion I did it as a bona fide member of the congregation, one of "them." I was taking part in their ceremony, the Mass, at which up to now I'd sat as a spectator. A strange word, Mass. It comes from the Latin *missa*, which means "dismissal" and as applied to the whole service is taken from the words *Ite, missa est*, "Go, you are dismissed," which the priest says near the end. (In the new English Mass the priest says, "The Mass is ended. Go in peace.") But I always found it hard to dissociate the word from its ordinary English meaning: something large, heavy, solid; while a friend tells me that she could never get used to the French word, *La Messe.*

Although I was never to become wholly adept at all the moves and pieces of timing that were second nature to my fellow worshipers I quite quickly mastered the basic tactics and procedures of the ceremony. I remember following the Mass in my missal a couple of weeks after my baptism and thinking that now I was doing it with near veteran or "professional" ease. Before that my missal, a handsome leather-bound one that had been given to me by Ruth, had at first seemed to be thoroughly alien and impenetrable and then, after she'd patiently gone through it with me, had begun to be comprehensible. Still it remained a disturbing object. Doubtless it could be a source of power and of liberating secrets, I thought, but there was also something adolescently arcane and even mumbo jumbo about it, as though it were a handbook for Masons or a Boy Scout manual.

Now I had learned to decipher it more or less, and felt more at ease, more like an initiate. Besides, I remember thinking, the Church *was* rather like the Masons or the Boy Scouts, if only in the sense that it too was a society or community with rules, precepts, ceremonies and stated values; the missal was then the handbook for this community's central ceremony and for its liturgical year. And yet there were times when the book's alien quality would strike my eyes again when I turned a page.

I reach for this missal, which has been for years on a high shelf in my library, and open it at random. Page 1625: at the bottom I see this:

First Vespers (October 17)
From the Common of Apostles, p. 1039.
    Collect as at Mass p. 1626
Commemoration of St. Margaret Mary Alacoque
    Ant. Veni sponsa p. 1112, Diffusa est, p. 1129.
    Collect as at Mass, p. 1622.

I remember how the typography often puzzled me and I remember too how the constant cross-references kept me frantically riffling back and forth. Nearly twenty-five years after I last used the missal I've forgotten most of its words, which are really the words of the Mass: Collect, Common, Veni sponsa. What do they mean? I sit here and think. Some fragments of meaning float back and then it all sinks again into the recesses of my memory.

At the time, though, knowing how to use the missal was one of the ways in which I had begun to fit in. And this produced complex feelings in me, ranging from sly pleasure at possessing a type of new semisecret identity to a sense of being an interloper despite the way I had taken my place among the faithful, or rather just because of that. I was fitting in, but this implied that I had come from elsewhere, had *been* someone else, and had arrived trailing differences which I would have to work in a strange, uncomfortable fashion to obliterate.

Yet why? What could I have expected in this regard? I was a convert and how would it be possible for me to erase the things that made me different from born Catholics for whom the Church was at the same time religion, background, community and, for better or worse, a chief principle of identity? And did I really want to erase these differences? To begin with I surely didn't want to erase my Jewishness. I had accepted the Church's argument that Catholicism was the fulfillment of Judaism, not its negation, and I didn't feel guilty of having "betrayed" anything. Besides, I'd become a Catholic from a stance of pure atheism, and hard as it might be to separate the ethnic and spiritual aspects of Judaism I'd already done it.

So I would remain Jewish, ethnically, or in the eyes of others. Which was just the point. For centuries being Jewish was regarded as both a religious and a racial matter, until the rise of secularism brought about a widespread abandonment of religious practice by Jews. How were they then to be identified except by their background? Frenchmen, Spaniards, Italians, Mexicans, and so on, have also in large numbers relinquished their religion in the modern age, but they're not stuck with being called Catholic; the religious term slides off them. One of the attractions of Catholicism had been its promise of an internationalism of the spirit, a loyalty surpassing race and culture, and I thought I could vault over ethnic differences on the wings of a transcendence; I thought I could adopt the Church as my true motherland.

For a while it worked. Beyond question it was a good thing that I began my life as a Catholic where I did. For the fact was that my fellow worshipers during this time were so unlike me racially and culturally, from such a different caste and world, that I felt relieved. I didn't have any need to compare myself to them the way I had to the secretaries and washerwomen and FBI types who made up nearly all the

Catholics I had ever seen and who, because they were from *my* society, my race and culture, lent themselves to my snobbery, my sense of intellectual superiority.

The truth was that I thought of these Mexican women and the few men who came to the church as being exotic in a way and I could accept them and even envy them their simplicity and what I took to be their innocence, qualities I wanted, with immense naïveté as it naturally turned out, to engender in myself. I felt inferior to them spiritually, and this had the odd result of putting me in the way of my feelings of being an interloper or impostor. I too was a believer now, all right, but I hadn't been one before, and so it was as if I had come uninvited by these people into their house, as the result of a whim for all they knew, into the house where they had always lived; God or the Holy Ghost may have asked me in, but *they* hadn't.

The central element of the Mass, the high point of its "drama" and purpose, is the Eucharist, Communion, and this was rather a problem for me from the start. During the months when I was looking on but hadn't yet become a Catholic I used to watch with fascination the people who went up to take Communion when that part of the service came round. I remember often thinking how heterogeneous they were, especially on Sundays, when I would go with Ruth.

I would see well-dressed couples, teenagers, a few children, shabby old women, cops, who knows maybe a doctor or a dentist or a construction worker here and there. And I would think about how the act of taking Communion seemed to fulfill its name by bringing them into an affinity and common identity, their differences of sex, age and class momentarily obliterated. I don't mean anything politically, or sociologically or even metaphysically romantic by this, their sharing, let's say, in some splendid principle of equality of a kind that operates nowhere else and so might be a model. Or it may be I thought something like this abstractly but it wasn't what I saw.

I would look at the faces of these people and watch the way they moved as they went toward the altar rail and again when they came back. There wasn't much difference between the way they looked on these two little journeys, except that everything was more pronounced on the return trip.

Almost all of them had roughly the same expression on their faces and almost all moved in one of only two ways. Usually their eyes were half closed or they stared straight ahead or at the floor. Their mouths were nearly always closed, but self-consciously so, especially as they walked back to their pews with the Communion wafers dissolving on their tongues. It gave them a somewhat grim or pursed appearance. They moved either stiffly, slowly, very much like sleepwalkers, or else they scurried, but abstractedly, as if they were hurrying through a landscape of which they took no notice.

It was as if they had all been stricken suddenly with the same, probably fatal, disease, or had witnessed the same grave or awful event, a sight that had made them dreamy or thoughtful or tense, because their responsibilities had been increased. They were *carrying* themselves, I remember thinking, which really meant that they were carrying, self-importantly or, more often, humbly, the wafer or the anticipation of it or the sense of it if they'd already swallowed. They were treating themselves as reliquaries. I couldn't imagine myself ever acting like them, looking as they did.

But when it came my turn I must have acted like them. During the first week after my baptism the day arrived when I would take Communion for the first time. Such a trivial physical act, I told myself as the moment drew near: a papery, ecru-colored wafer deposited on your tongue by a priest who often had to conduct the whole operation as though on an assembly line, moving mechanically down the row of kneeling worshipers, placing the Host in the successively opened mouths, and intoning the accompanying little prayer, "May the body and blood of our Lord Jesus Christ lead you to life everlasting," or something like that.

I told myself that it wasn't complicated, that it was simply food for the soul, but I was apprehensive anyway. I can't remember which of two extreme conditions I was in as I moved for the first time from my pew to the aisle and then down to the altar rail. Either I was in complete turmoil or, more likely, I had emptied myself of all thought and emotion and moved down the aisle, knelt at the altar like the others (there were perhaps a dozen women and a few men), heard without registering the priest's words—but now, abruptly, I remember them precisely: "May the body of our Lord Jesus Christ preserve thy soul to life everlasting"—and received the thing in my mouth in a state of near catatonia.

I have just called the Host a "thing," which at the very least is disrespectful. But all the time I was a believer I was never able to call it anything else, certainly not "Host," for that was a word that puzzled and for some reason irritated me, as a number of other Catholic words and phrases did, simply as language: Sacred Heart, sodality, novena, Offertory. More fundamentally I could never wholly get over a deep mistrust of this central aspect of Catholic belief and practice, a mistrust to which was added a strain of embarrassment. I could never really accept, no matter how hard I tried (and I did try; I worked at it furiously), that what I was swallowing was in fact the "body" and by implication the "blood" of Christ.

If it had simply been a matter of symbolic substance and action, as I'm sure most open-minded people outside the

Church consider it to be, if it had been a matter of representation, I could have managed it without difficulty. After all, I knew about symbolic modes and actions, from literature most comfortably; I knew about metaphor. But "transubstantiation," the word that describes the phenomenon of the Eucharist, the consumption of the Host and its subsequent effect, isn't a metaphor; it doesn't refer to something *standing for* something else, but to a materialization in another form or appearance, literally a "crossing-over" of substance.

And so this is what I faced: what I took in and ingested was and wasn't the body and blood of Christ. It wasn't, because all that was in your mouth was this papery object that dissolved very quickly and left scarcely any taste. And it was, because the Faith held it to be and you weren't supposed to rely on your senses or your reason in a matter such as this. It was a mystery, one of the many that resided at the center of belief, from which indeed belief hung; they would strain your mind to the breaking point if you chased after them, or they would induce humility and acceptance if you gave up the need for thoroughly rational explanation and simply let them be.

As long as I was an active Catholic I wavered or shuttled between these two opposing attitudes toward the Host and Communion and was more often in the condition of beleaguered doubt, my brain thumping with the effort to understand how this bizarre notion could be true and to learn the proper spirit in which it ought to be accepted. I spoke earlier of wanting mystery, and I stand by that. But in this case, as in some others, the mystery seemed too literal, if I can put it that way; unlike the idea of eternal happiness in God's bosom or Christ's redemptive sacrifice, its mysteriousness was confined to a physical fact, a thing being said to be another thing.

I remember at first making a grotesque attempt to cut

round the perplexity by imagining literal flesh and blood in my mouth, which naturally disgusted me and made me realize that whatever else was going on here the Church was civilized enough not to ask us to pretend to be cannibals.

After that I went back to the idea of symbolic representation, knowing that this wasn't it either. But at least here I was helped by the fact that once I started to receive Communion the act and process immediately connected itself to the idea of the Mystical Body, which, with Christ at the center, was composed of all believers and which you entered or joined as soon as you had swallowed the wafer. Or so I understood the notion at the time.

The idea of a *body* of mankind, a close unity of all human beings, was familiar enough as a secular metaphor, a political one, for example. And so I didn't have all that much difficulty in taking the next mental step, accepting the unity that common belief in Christ forged and seeing it as something more than an idea. It was a *mystical* body, after all, I remember telling myself, it wasn't to be thought of in literal ways. Even so I would find myself trying to imagine it as somehow palpable, alternately envisaging it as a gigantic skin in which we were all encased or as a warm Jell-O-like sea in which we floated side by side, all of us, men, women, children, babies, along with the peaceful dead.

And so I had trouble from the beginning. There were times, though, when doubt would drop away and I would feel myself yielding to the sacrament and even feeling, or thinking that I did, its efficacy spreading through me. And always, however clumsily or heatedly I struggled with the idea of the Eucharist and other dogmas or beliefs—the Immaculate Conception, the Virgin Birth, Original Sin, the Trinity, Papal Infallibility and so on—all the doctrines and propositions that anti-Catholics can't stomach and that I too once couldn't abide—I understood and welcomed the way in which they made Catholicism different from any other religion I knew about. (Later I learned that the Episcopal and Lutheran churches accept most of these doctrines too.) Most important of all, I relied on the manner in which these dogmas and teachings separated the Faith from the nonreligious, untranscendent, rationalistic approaches to our lives and the world that I had previously explored and to which at times had committed myself.

I remember that after I had begun to be interested in Catholicism I came upon Saint Paul's definition of faith as "the evidence of things unseen" and thought the contradiction ought to be especially appealing to those who loved literature. In the same vein I remember being excited by Charles Péguy's description of the "bourgeois mind" as that which, whatever the person's social or economic class, invariably "preferred the visible to the invisible." I thought this the most acute and witty indictment of the materialist I'd ever seen, unless it was Baudelaire's epithet: "fanatics of utensils, enemies of perfume."

In the realm of aesthetics I had loved art in both particular works and as a category, because I had always wanted to believe in the invisible, to be in touch with a reality beyond the actual. When, in Kierkegaard's sense, I moved from a world of aesthetic truth to one of religion I of course wanted such a reality too. It was in fact one of the sources of my difficulty with so many practices of the Church that in them the attempt was always being made to convert the invisible into the visible, an action I thought resulted in a loss of mystery together with a plague of vulgarity: the Sacred Hearts, the Shroud of Turin, weeping Madonnas and all the relics.

Yet I had been guilty of that myself (the sea of Jell-O!) as an act of rebellion against the transcendence I otherwise craved and as something more: a periodic desire for specificity, the tangible in a world of abstraction. I had been attracted to Catholicism in part because of its efforts to bridge such gaps and fuse such antinomies and, in a more accepting mood, I could see that Communion, for example, was a way of bringing together physical and spiritual realities in an attempt to assuage what many people, religiously inclined or not, have always felt to be an intolerable space between facts and values.

In the midst of my rapacious purity of mental desire (I think of Blake's poem) I could see that for the Church to try to make certain aspects of the spirit and its operations palpable, or give them a visual correlative, wasn't necessarily to be vulgar or dim-witted or bourgeois in the sense of Péguy's criticism, but to offer a concession to our limitations. It was a way of dealing with our inability ever truly to grasp the spiritual except as somehow incarnate, clothed. Christ, who was God but also man, might be thought of as the supreme example of that concession.

Later I would again rebel against the literalism of Catholic cults and popular practices but for now I went on the understanding that if anything distinguished Catholicism it was that it had never rested on abstractions, certainly not simple ethical ones, the way much of Protestantism does, but continually sank the realm of values back into the living bodies and textures of the world. So I swallowed my doubts along with the wafer and went to Communion nearly every day for several months and then two or three times a week, and after that once a week or so for a year or two and then less and less frequently as my faith dwindled. Never wholly able to give myself over to the sacrament, I managed, I thought, to fit within its spirit.

Moving on. In order to be eligible for Communion you aren't supposed to have any mortal sins on your conscience, which means that in the linked series of actions and events of which Catholic practice is made up, Confession is obligatory at least once a year for everyone, even the most saintly, for even they don't escape entirely the effects of Original Sin. Confession: the word has such different associations for me as I write this from what it had when the sacrament greatly affected my behavior and ruled my moral self.

I glance over at my bookshelves, at a section containing miscellaneous books that have come to me from one source or another and that I don't intend to read or keep but haven't got round yet to disposing of. Among them are a number of "confessional" works, the tale of a movie star's flamboyant past, the revelations of a tennis star which include an account of her lesbian affair.

The word "confess" is of French origin, by way of Latin, where its components have the literal meaning of "to speak" or "declare" or "assert" to or with another person or persons. How it came to refer for several centuries almost exclusively to avowals of guiltiness I haven't been able to learn, but that it's come in recent years to apply to the blabbing of all one's ostensible secrets seems obviously to have to do with the great weakening in our time of the boundaries between the public and the private, which used to be more clearly demarcated. Anyway, the link between the word's original secular and religious uses is clear when we speak of confessing to a crime.

In Catholic Confession one naturally doesn't speak to just anyone or declare something to the world-at-large, trying to garner as many listeners as possible, but to one person, who may be said to represent everyone else but also God, and who is sworn to secrecy. And this person is, usually, hidden or screened from the penitent (the word suggests sackcloth and ashes and staggeringly heavy crosses carried by fanatic Mexican peasants but all it really means in regard to Confession is that you have to be in a penitential or remorseful frame of mind if the process is to work) in a kind of shadowy wooden box standing on end, one of which containers I approached for the first time a couple of days after my baptism.

I remember being in a state of minor trepidation, most likely because of the sheer unfamiliarity of it, but nothing like serious alarm. There was even a sense in which I rather looked forward to the experience. Having read so much of Freud (for a time I had kept above my desk a photograph of the famous couch in his Vienna consulting room) and having even had a little psychotherapy myself, I didn't find particularly unsettling the prospect of talking about intimate matters to a stranger.

Besides, the priest who had baptized me had given me careful instructions in the procedure and had even rehearsed it with me. You go in, kneel down on the prie-dieu on your side of the partition, begin by saying "Bless me, Father, for I have sinned," go on to say, "Since my last Confession I've committed the following sins . . ." and so on, or rather, for this one occasion in my case, "This is my first Confession" (suppressing the impulse to add, "You see, Padre, until just the other day I was a Jewish atheist humanist") and wait for the presence on the other side to respond.

That ear on the other side of the grillwork. As I say, I wasn't at all abashed at the necessity of speaking intimately to this unknown person, unknown, that's to say, in his life and thoughts and what he might share with you or not share, beyond your mutual faith. Besides, I didn't have very much of anything in the way of the intimate to report that day.

You could of course learn quite a bit about a confessor if you kept going back to him and you could always learn his name and a few details of his history and status, especially if you were going to Confession in a small church with only one or two priests, which is all this one had. I think the one I went to that first time was named Sanchez, a man I'd seen celebrating Mass, but he blurs with later confessors in my mind and might have been named Sullivan; there are swarthy, Latin-looking Irishmen.

For some time I didn't trouble myself about the particular priest to whom I was confessing, since as far as I consciously knew I fully accepted the instrumental nature of the ritual or sacrament, having been taught that it didn't matter what the priest's own spiritual condition was, because the putative grace and forgiveness passed through him, as it were, in his go-between or emissary-like role as God's agent. (Greene's whiskey priest could say Mass and perform other sacred acts; the gap between his degradation and his formal role as God's deputy is one thing that gives *The Power and the Glory* its taut sadness.) Nor did it matter what his intellectual attributes were, the level of his moral perception, say, or his awareness of psychological complexity.

Later on this would begin to be important to me but at this point I didn't give it much thought. If anything, I carried my romanticism over to the matter, wanting, as I remember it, a priest with a simple heart, an uncomplicated mind, someone on the model of the country curate of Bernanos's novel. I certainly didn't want any reformers at this time, any Christian firebrands.

Just before I stepped for the first time into the "Box," as I'd heard Catholics refer to it, I remember thinking that it had some physical or rather atmospheric resemblance to the orgone box of Wilhelm Reich, in one of which, a friend's, I had once sat for some minutes, with no observable result. It was about five o'clock on a Saturday afternoon now, the usual time for confessions in most Catholic churches. It was already dark outside. I took my place at the end of a line composed mainly of elderly women, some of whom were murmuring prayers and fingering their rosary beads with their eyes closed. I wondered what sort of sins they could have on their consciences.

When my turn came I walked gingerly into the gloomy enclosure, knelt down in the semidarkness and began the words of the ritual. I sensed rather than saw the priest on the other side and heard him cough once. When I was finished and he finally spoke to me it was in a tired, noncommittal voice and he made no reference to the fact that it was my first Confession, which I had thought would have interested him. For a moment I knelt there in annoyance, resentful that he didn't seem to have the faintest interest in me, until I remembered that I was probably the tenth or twentieth sinner he had had to listen to that day.

In any case I wasn't much of a sinner at the moment, so I only spent his time, not his psychic strength. I didn't have anything at all grave or startling to lay before him. The flesh had been unprecedentedly quiet for some time now, I wasn't ridden just then with malice or vicious with envy, nor was I acting slothful in any way I could determine. When I walked out I quickly said the two Hail Marys he had given me as a penance for the trifling misdemeanors I had confided in him only because I thought I ought to offer something. I remember thinking it rather peculiar to be ordered to say a prayer for a penance—a greeting to the Virgin as a penalty?—but I shrugged and said it all the same.

This priest was fairly typical in the light penance he gave me. Seldom during my years as a Catholic was I asked to do much more than that, even when I had far more serious matters to confess. But against the popular notion outside the Church that Confession actually *keeps* people sinning, since you walk in, get absolved and are then free to go back to whatever vices you habitually practice, I found that having to confess indeed made it harder for me to sin, as the ritual is intended to do.

This clearly had nothing to do with any fear of a heavy penance. It stemmed from the fact that I knew I wasn't really talking to the priest in the box but through him; I knew that he was a channel to God's ear, and as long as I believed in God I literally didn't want to offend Him. Sin is an offense against God, almost always committed against His creatures, which is what distinguishes it from crime or general immorality. And for a long time the thought of offending Him, after what my experience of His special concern for me had been, troubled me greatly and served to keep me from indulging in certain vices far more often than I would otherwise have been likely to do. After a while it got more complicated.

There was one more matter to deal with and that was the problem presented to me by the prohibition against eating meat on Fridays—a ban that wasn't lifted for American Catholics until some years after I'd stopped going to church—and, when my first one came round, fasting during Lent. As I would learn later, there were many Catholics, vegetarians or lovers of fish and seafood, for whom the rule offered no difficulties whatsoever, but for me it was a real hardship. I loved meat and detested fish, a loathing whose origin no doubt lay in my childhood, from which there would periodically emerge memories of the iodine smell given off by the mackerel or halibut or whatever kind of fish it was that my mother, poor soul suffering from the twin afflictions of the Depression economy and the most proletarian of culinary backgrounds, would so often serve, almost always boiled or at any rate without sauce or any embellishment whatever.

Tuna fish was close enough to meat, so I would often eat

that on Fridays, or else I'd have spaghetti with garlic and butter or macaroni and cheese or maybe garden vegetables with sour cream. All in all Fridays were never that bad but when my first Lent began a week or so after I got back to New York, my ingenuity began to be severely taxed and before a week of the six had passed I felt as though no member of the flock was being more profoundly tested than I was, that I was the exemplary target of the proscription.

Before that first Lent, during the month or so I remained in Colorado Springs, I did have a problem with dinner at my friends' house on Fridays. It happened that Grove hated fish even more passionately than I did—I had once heard him swear that he would never eat anything that had been underwater for more than ten minutes in its life—and was a great enthusiast of beef, pork, and so on. If I remember it rightly I handled the business by begging off on a couple of Fridays and on the others going over and pleading lack of appetite due to some minor indisposition.

And so on the whole my life was surprisingly satisfying during this period, considering how violent had been the upheaval, the snapped roots and greatly altered sense of the world and my possible place in it. Or so I've often thought as I look back on it. There aren't many times in one's adult life when everything is in its place, lucid, bounded, and free from painful desire, when everything is clarity and regular movement, as my life was then.

The way I lived was exceedingly simple and precisely organized, as though I were stepping along under an invisible military discipline, a regimen silently laid out; I had the most modest of places in a hierarchy and was content with it. More than this, or more likely as a result of it, my life was almost entirely free of temptations, both of an immediate physical and, above all, sexual kind, and the more abstract pull of ambition, the solicitation by the world to make a name for myself, to be *somebody*.

Colorado Springs wasn't yet the site of the Air Force Academy. It was at a high altitude and was a quiet, extraordinarily clean place, considerably well-to-do as far as I could tell, genteel and rather cultivated, as the presence of the art museum testified. Up above on a mountainside was the Broadmoor, a fantastically huge resort hotel that I never visited but used to think of as looking like Kafka's Castle. Winter in the shadow of Pikes Peak was exhilarating, crystalline. I remember how I loved battling the air, the drawstring of my parka pulled tight and my hands kept warm in ratty fur-lined gloves from the Salvation Army store. A sudden snowstorm might blow down off the mountains, leaving everything when it ended silent and serene.

And so for that month or more I was content to live in this undemanding place, with a fine, welcome asceticism, on my tiny salary, without ambition and with my gaze fixed in the general direction of Heaven. But after a while, as might have been predicted, I began to be afflicted with two kinds of itching: temptations stirred, a slight reassertion of my literary ambitions and a tic, then an outbreak, of generalized erotic longing.

For as long as I was in Colorado I was able to suppress the desire to write, through a series of informal meditations on the vanity of worldly hungers (how archaic those words came to seem to me!), along with a rereading of that preeminent guidebook to asceticism and humility, the *Imitation of Christ*. But the sexual desire, after having been squelched so thoroughly and for so long, now began to press me, at first in sudden sneaky appearances in my head, images of bodies and acts, and then more deliberately, set off by the sight of an alluring woman in the street or by a magazine photo of some stirring kind; and these occasions of carnal imagination grew more frequent and intense.

I didn't know any women socially—my friends' friends were almost all young married couples like themselves—and Colorado Springs didn't seem to have any underlife that I could discover. So one Saturday morning after Mass, very much aware of the deception or hypocrisy I was practicing, I ate breakfast and got in my car to drive up to Denver, some eighty miles away. There I spent most of the afternoon and evening prowling through the tenderloin district, or what a cabdriver had told me might be regarded as one, in a fruitless search for a prostitute I probably wouldn't have been able to afford anyway. Back in my room in the Springs late that night I allowed sexual fantasies to take hold with only a trace of opposition and gave myself over to masturbation for the first time in many months.

It was my first real sin as a Catholic, certainly my first "mortal" one. At last, I thought, I've got something to confess, but it also meant that the next morning I'd have to forgo Communion for the first time, since I obviously couldn't get to Confession before then. Beyond such considerations was the fact of how I felt, and would have felt, I think, whether I was Catholic or not. When I finished doing it I experienced a swift rush of loneliness, emptiness really, a common result of masturbation—the sense of sterility and the solipsism that are suggested by the biblical "spilling of one's seed upon the ground"—and I knew then that it was time for me to go home.

By home I of course meant New York, although no family or apartment awaited me there. (Later my wife and I would come back together for a time, but for now we remained wholly apart.) But New York was where I belonged and where I knew my life would have to be, in that future which presented no details to my imagination, not the sketchiest scenario, but simply existed as the next phase, the site of the steps I would take after the recent ones.

In a way I would be going back like an internal immigrant, like one of those thousands of young people from all over the country who, as high schools and colleges let out every May and June, follow an arc of ambition to that city where things are known to begin to happen. The difference was that as far as I consciously knew I wasn't seeking to start or advance a career as much as I was looking for a milieu in the midst of which I might discover what to expect, what I could or should do.

And so one evening at the beginning of February I had my last dinner with the Groves and said good-bye, thanking them for all their kindnesses and keeping my secret from them still. The next morning I went to the earliest Mass, ate breakfast, settled with the landlady and got in my car to start out. On the radio there were storm warnings for eastern Colorado and western Kansas and I knew how devastating winter on the plains could be. So on the spur of the moment I decided not to drive straight across the country to New York, where nothing pressing awaited me in any case, but to go southeast, to Oklahoma City, as my road map suggested, with the intention of continuing on into Texas, then across to New Orleans and after that on north.

I'd saved a little money and had gotten some from my parents, enough altogether to let me stay for a while in New Orleans, an idea that came to me as I drove. I had passed through the city a few years before when I was hitchhiking to Mexico (my God, how fearless I once was!) but I hadn't really seen it. What I had noticed was a surface of gaudy nightlife and some architectural vestiges of European culture, but it had been enough to make me think of it as a rather mysterious, funky place. I also knew that it was one of the most Catholic cities in America, along with Boston I supposed, and this appealed to me too.

As I raced at ninety miles an hour along the straight and all but deserted highway out of Colorado Springs I remember thinking that I had moved from one minority to another, except that I had joined this one, the Catholic, by an act that left me superficially indistinguishable from what I'd been before and from everyone else and I was aware that Catholics were much the largest minority and the most integrated into the texture of American life.

Oh, I knew that the Ku Klux Klan had been organized nearly a century ago almost as much against Catholics as against blacks and Jews, and that in the South and much of the Midwest, anti-Catholicism was still in place. Nevertheless, I thought, to be Catholic in America, in most regions anyway, wasn't nearly as oppressive as being Jewish; there wasn't the same depth to the stain with which you were covered, the shudder you might cause in the natives wasn't nearly so involuntary.

Well I wasn't about to declare myself a Jewish Catholic on the courthouse steps of southern towns or in general stores in Indiana. And anyway I wasn't concerned at the time about how I'd be regarded or treated by strangers but about my own perspective, how I'd feel in a city like New Orleans, what being Catholic would be like in a Catholic place. There would be time enough to see how I'd feel among Protestants and religious nondescripts, to see how different my attitudes might have become from the position of alienation and opposition, intellectual and cultural far more than ethnic or religious (or so I told myself), that I had had before.

This was all very abstract, a sociology class, as I remember it now. The reality was that as evening came I stopped for the night in Oklahoma City, a raw ugly place with oil derricks I could see from my downtown hotel window. At the back of my mind for several days had been the thought that I might find a prostitute in one of the cities along my route. For years I had had visions of certain alluring American cities I'd never been to; mainly in the South and West, they were "open," full of a powerful, dangerous sexuality, a frontier eroticism. And so when the bellboy had switched on the lights in my room and inquired into any other "needs" I might have, I responded with an alacrity that seemed to startle him.

But when I answered the knock at my door later that night I was dismayed to see a girl who couldn't have been more than seventeen, a skinny creature with dull red hair and a bad complexion, the complete antithesis of my sexual ideal. So I mumbled an apology, gave her some money and after she'd gone lay down on the bed to try, futilely as it turned out, to summon up images I might be aroused by, after having arranged in my head for a provisional indulgence from God based on the rigors of my long period of celibacy.

The next morning I drove down to Dallas. It was such a clean and sterile city, alarming in its coldness and silences. On an impulse of absurd homesickness I decided to have dinner in a Jewish delicatessen, which advertised itself as the only one south (or was it west) of somewhere, and was amused and slightly appalled by the tall, rawboned waitresses shouting orders for pastrami on rye and matzoh-ball soup in their Texas drawls and twangs.

I got up early the next morning and drove east, through Beaumont, on into Louisiana and after a night in, I think, Alexandria, across a bridge into New Orleans. Was it called the Huey P. Long Memorial Bridge, or did I see that name, a dangerous exotic one from my childhood, on some other public project? The name of the lake was Pontchartrain, which was exotic enough.

I had decided to find a rooming house, so I parked somewhere downtown—it was Saturday—and had breakfast while I looked through the classifieds in the delightfully named *Times-Picayune*. One ad caught my eye. It was from a woman who said she was a widow with a couple of "cheerful" rooms to rent, adding that her house was "near Catholic churches." I got directions to the address, which turned out to be not very far from Canal Street, parked in front of a ramshackle old house with some flaking pillars, spoke to the landlady, who wasn't precisely a motherly type, as the one in Colorado Springs had been, and who seemed somewhat suspicious of my New York license plates and accent, and rented a large, rather gloomy room with a heavy comforter on the bed which I was sure I wasn't going to need.

It was astonishingly warm for February, even in so southerly a city as this, I thought. The air was sticky and, the word came into my head as I was taking a walk that evening, full of decay. Yes, there was the smell of rot everywhere, the sick-sweet odor of things decomposing. It came of course from the heavy vegetation, the catalpa and palmetto trees, the Spanish moss and honeysuckle and other flowering shrubs I couldn't name. But this didn't account for all of it. It seemed to me as I walked toward the center of town on this Saturday evening that something noxious was seeping from the life here, an exudation of tainted mortality. What could have made me think or rather physically detect this? A police car screaming down an avenue, a crippled black man swigging from a pint bottle as he limped along? Merely the heat? I knew it was foolish.

And then I came at length to Bourbon Street, astounding

in its concentrated glitter and buzz of, what seemed to me in my high-mindedness, depravity, the neon, the music roaring from open doorways (some of it jazz, of course, and some of that fine; I stopped for a time to watch and listen at Preservation Hall), the gaudy postered nudes, the prostitutes ambling along and swinging huge purses—that odd detail stays in my mind—and I thought again that the city was a place of death, that it was like Venice in Mann's story.

But I was fascinated too. I stepped into a bar where a sinewy blond woman in a G-string was writhing on a platform between the sides of the horseshoe-shaped counter. As I sat and watched her, nursing a beer, a strapping dark-haired woman sat down in a seat next to me and began propositioning me in a voice whose huskiness and southern indolence quickly made me ripe for surrender. After a while we left the bar and went to a hotel a couple of blocks away where I enacted the ritual of submissiveness that made up one side of my sexual nature.

She was a friendly woman named Ruby (I thought it perfect) and so, out of loneliness and against my usual practice of bolting in shame and self-loathing after an episode with a whore, I asked her if she'd like to go for a drink. No, she told me, it was after midnight and she wanted to fast so as to be able to go to Communion in the morning. So elastic a species of Catholic morality was startlingly new to me, but I didn't think her hypocritical.

The next morning I went to a church near my rooming house. My own morality didn't permit me the faintest thought of taking Communion, but I didn't want to compound the sin by missing Mass. It was Sunday and I went to High Mass. I'd never been bothered much by incense before but now it came wafting through the nondescript church filled with the usual tacky art and votive gewgaws and mingled with the mustiness all churches seem to produce, to make up a smell I found almost too much to bear. Afterward I walked for a while, trying to shake off the depression I felt.

At an intersection I suddenly came upon a streetcar with a destination sign reading DESIRE. It had only been a few years since the play had made such a sensation in New York, where I had seen it, and my first reaction now was one of delighted recognition. But then as I walked I began to think of Williams's whole array of images of death and corruption, which I realized I had been unconsciously calling on in my thoughts the previous evening about a city where the plague reigned. My mood of dislocation and despair deepened and I couldn't fathom its causes.

When I got back to my room I knew there was one thing I could do to combat my dark spirits, so I set up my typewriter on a little table and got to work. I started by writing a line or two of poetry, then switched to putting down notes and phrases for a story about . . . it comes back to me now, about a man who aches for love but finds degradation instead. (It's a good thing I didn't get very far with it.)

I stayed in New Orleans for nearly two weeks, until my money began to run out, spending the time exploring the city and writing in my room, but I was never able to get free of the mingled sadness and anxiety I felt there, which mood was in such contrast to the calmness and psychic solidity I'd known in Colorado Springs. And all this time I was trying to understand the change. The incident with the prostitute was more symptom than cause, and in any case I'd gone to Confession soon afterward and—though not only for that reason—was almost free of sexual longing once more.

Then I began to figure it out. It was that in Colorado I had at least had my friends and a job and had been sustained by the new regimen of my life as a Catholic and by something more subtle: the relief, the lightness that came from having brought to a denouement a long period of spiritual uncertainty and struggle. But here, away from the scene of my "accident" and recuperation, I felt entirely displaced, bereft; and the Church, which I had been thinking of as a "home," didn't feel at all like one now.

When I tried to pray it was with a sort of gasp, as though I couldn't get enough air or, to change the metaphor, it was as if I were marooned on an island and was pleading for the sight of a ship on the horizon. I knew that prayer wasn't supposed to be a means to fulfill wishes, above all immediate material ones—even for health—but a conduit to another dimension, a movement past one's "situation." But for me now it was almost wholly a plea for relief.

"Get me out of here," I was saying beneath the formal words, the "here" meaning this city I had with extravagant romanticism transformed into a kind of Sodom, and also the condition of alienation to which, for the first time since my baptism, I dimly saw the Church as contributing instead of assuaging. What I didn't understand until quite awhile later was that I had created a confusion of realms (which would be the title of my first book, on very different subjects from this, some years later): I wanted the Faith to work psychologically at every moment, in the here and now; I wasn't prepared for the actuality of loneliness and estrangement, its feeling in the body of icy oceans and failing breath, something the Church, religion, might validate as proper to fallen mankind, might explain or promise eventual succor from, but never, while we live, cure.

In opposite ways, I came later to realize, my months in Colorado Springs and the two weeks in New Orleans had both been unreal, the one sojourn secure in its artificial boundedness, the other immensely slippery, providing no ground at all. And what could I have expected? Why should being a Catholic have made me more at home anywhere, or at least less ambiguous in my relations to people and places? All I knew at the time, though, was that I had to get back to New York, where I could begin to see how my life in the world might mesh with my new faith. So one night I packed up, put everything I'd written in a manila envelope—the fragments of poetry, the scraps of reflection, the abortive stories, all the notes that hadn't been transformed into *writing*—and the next morning paid my bill and left.

I drove the thirteen hundred miles with furious, single-minded intensity, stopping only for quick meals and once for a couple of hours of sleep in some woods beside a road in Georgia or Tennessee, and got into New York over the George Washington Bridge late on the second evening. I'd called a cousin of mine, Elliott Echelman, who told me I could stay with him and his roommate for a while, so I went to his place, a cold-water flat on Eighth Avenue, and after some disjointed conversation fell asleep on a sofa in the tiny living room. The next morning I went over to St. Malachy's, a little church known as the Actors' Chapel because it's in the heart of the theater district on Forty-ninth Street, knelt in a pew near the back and, my mind spinning with disorder, self-pity and hope, burst into tears.

Mystery ↓

Chapter 3

FROM THE MOMENT I GOT BACK TO NEW YORK I RE-covered the morale of Colorado Springs. Being Catholic excited me again, the sense of estrangement I'd felt in New Orleans was gone. Oh, I certainly didn't fit back into anything, I didn't have anyplace to go back to filling. But just to have around me the city where I'd been born and grown up, to have all the familiarity of street signs and house fronts and public noises, *The Times* again and WQXR, the subway and Joe's dinette on Fourth Street, gave my body and my senses the comfort they'd recently lacked. As for my spirit it rose again, perhaps just because it had stopped being in conflict with my physical situation. Going to church now, or praying, was more like it had been before: adventurous, mysteriously fecund, not desperate or compensatory.

I skated over the next week or two as though on a Rocke-feller Center rink of the mind. But then from the realm of the practical came an announcement: you need a job. And so, more because I had absolutely no material skills or training, having been educated haphazardly in what we like to call the liberal arts, than out of a direct ambition toward journalism or publishing, I called upon the one dubious asset I possessed —literacy—and wrote identical letters to some forty book publishers and magazine editors, asking them for an interview.

I got only three replies, two of them from publishers. One of them was Helen Wolff, who was at Pantheon then, I believe, and who was extraordinarily kind to me, on this occasion and later; she told me that she'd liked my letter but that alas, or *ach*, she had no job to offer. And then there was Time, Inc., publisher of *Time* and *Life;* someone in personnel also liked my letter and granted me an interview.

A tall, thin, bespectacled, youngish man from the personnel department quizzed me for over an hour, or rather engaged me in a sprawling, animated conversation about books, art and ideas. He was surprisingly literate (I suppose that like most intellectuals of my kind I'd thought of anyone who worked for Henry Luce as hopelessly square) and seemed pleased with our talk. I left with a promise that they'd get in touch with me and when they did I was told that they were "impressed" with me but that they considered me "too old" for *Life* and "too young" for *Time*. How about *Fortune?* I thought of writing them to ask.

The letter I had written to all these prospective and unlikely employers was, as I remember it now, a strange, naive declaration of my "commitment" to literature and belief in its humanizing power; I think I quoted Victor Hugo: "Literature is civilization itself." The whole document was likely to have struck most readers as having been composed by a teenager with dazzled eyes instead of by a man nearly in his thirties. In writing it I had had, as it were, to reconstruct my passion for literature, to depict it from memory and, remaining within the fiction of its present power over me, disguise the fact that journalism or editing was never going to appease it. For at the moment I was determined not to let my hopes for a literary career molest or undermine what I thought of as my spiritual task and program.

The writing I had done, or tried to do, in New Orleans had been a temporary relapse, I told myself. That it had been undertaken out of anxiety and had come to nothing had to be seen as a demonstration that whatever might become true in the future, serious writing wasn't what I ought to be doing right now. So I allowed this chastening to work on me. Looked at realistically though, the whole thing was academic, since nobody seemed to want my intellectual services, no matter how modest these might be, and I was fast running out of money.

It's a winter afternoon, growing dark, a few weeks after I'd come back to New York. I've been visiting a friend who lives in the eighties near Third Avenue and now am walking toward a bus stop to go back down to where I'm staying. On the spur of the moment I decide to get the crosstown bus first and so I shift my steps. This takes me past a bookstore I'd browsed in a couple of times before I'd gone to Colorado, a Catholic shop called the Paraclete, which means, I know, the Holy Spirit, in the special sense of comforter or intercessor. (Or perhaps I only learned that later.) It occurs to me as I go by that the two young women who own and run the place are the only Catholics I know in New York, except for Father Walsh and Ruth. But for some reason I don't want to see him right now and she, whom I do want to see, has disappeared.

I retrace my steps and walk into the store. It's cheerful and well lighted (or am I confusing it with a later place they had on Seventy-third?) and full of surprises compared with other Catholic bookshops I'd been in. Though I can see some black Bibles and missals and a number of gloomy-looking tomes and tracts, many of the books and pamphlets, which, I have time to notice, include a number of far-from-routine volumes of philosophy and social studies, are in bright covers and are attractively displayed.

Most of the devotional objects of art and use—statuettes,

crucifixes, paintings, candles and so on—are in a clean, un-kitschy style, a long way from the maudlin and emotionally rococo modes of conventional Catholic artifacts, though they wouldn't have caused a ripple in the wider world of taste. Though there are some unpleasant examples of mawkish Catholic objects, too, I decide they're around as a concession to commercial necessity. The store certainly wasn't promoting revolution, but I could imagine some eyebrows being raised at the sight of a stack of *Catholic Worker*s on a stand.

The women remember me and since it's not a busy time in the store we begin to talk. Before I know it I've unloaded my story on them, the whole tale of my conversion and its aftermath, winding up with my present desperate jobless-ness. The women are fascinated, sympathetic and, something I detect without wanting or being able to articulate it to myself at the time, *gratified*. This is the first time I've encountered such a reaction to my conversion on the part of Catholics (not that there had been all that many who knew my story during these weeks) but I was to meet with it on a number of occasions over the next few years.

What did this satisfaction at hearing of my conversion really mean to these women, who had known of my interest in the Church from my earlier visits to their shop? As I think back on it now it seems to me that the pleasure I saw in their faces and demeanor came from something having been worked out against the odds, from their having seen a divine plan, a lordly schema, in operation. It was as though my conversion was gratifying to them—and I ought to say that their responses were all low-key: quiet smiles, their heads nodding mildly—because it was exemplary of the way things ought to be. I was to come upon this attitude again and again: if everything was as it should be in the human world, such Catholics seemed to imply, then everyone would belong to the Church: Protestants, Jews, pagans, infidels and the dreamers of humanism. But of course they knew as I did that everything wasn't right, most certainly Catholics themselves.

The women showed me nothing like satisfaction in another soul having been "saved," another sinner plucked from perdition; there wasn't anything like the elation that revivalists seem so self-justifyingly to feel in the presence of a new convert: "We're roping them in, we *must* be right!" Neither of the women had anything of the proselyte about her and indeed the younger one, Joan Paul (the older's name was Elizabeth Sullivan), had a slight streak of irreverence, faintly touched with bitterness, I remember thinking. Whatever it was, she said things to me like, "Ooooh, you're in for it now!" and "Boy, you should have kept running."

So they didn't shout or whisper "hallelujah" nor did they welcome me with fuss into the company of the faithful as though I had been lost in the jungle and had staggered bleeding and haggard into their camp. They were much too intelligent and sophisticated for that. In the face of my lingering idea of Catholics as stuck in the intellectual and social past, mired in the prosaic if not in anything worse, I saw them as "advanced." Which to be sure was a relative matter, but everything testified to their not being in the business of dispensing piety, or mindless piety at any rate.

I inferred from all this and from their benign response when I mentioned Greene and Mauriac as having been among my influences, that they were on the right side of a dividing line I had for a long time been half-consciously setting up in my mind. At least they knew, I told myself, that the Church wasn't a solution to anybody's "identity crisis" or a redemption from one's "failure." It was a problematic and beleaguered enterprise that had a lot of work to do in its own social and intellectual backyards and, as custodian of the spirit and exponent of its proper choices, was as likely to bring new suffering as it was to assuage the old.

But we certainly didn't talk about anything so subtle and thorny at the time. After I had wound up my narrative they addressed themselves with fine practicality to my immediate situation. I had told them about my wacky and fruitless letter campaign for a job and now one of them turned to the other and said, "What about *Jubilee*?" This, it turned out, was a small new "liberal" Catholic monthly that had recently been started by two college friends of Thomas Merton, about whose connection to my conversion I had of course told the women.

Before I left the store I glanced over a copy of the magazine, which struck me as being visually a smaller *Life* or *Look*, where in fact its editor, Edward Rice, had worked. The women promised to call *Jubilee* the next morning, after which I was to call too. As I walked toward the bus stop I remember shaking my head over the continuing mad role Catholic bookstores and libraries were playing in my life. The next day I called Ed Rice and he asked me to come down. A few days after that I joined the magazine.

Before it became widely known that a number of priests and nuns were taking the side of peasants and workers in the bitter social struggles of South America, the phrase "left-wing" Catholicism would have struck most Americans as a contradiction in terms. Yet such a thing has existed throughout the century in Europe and, though on a smaller scale, for almost all that time here. At the time I went to work for *Jubilee* in 1954 there was a thin but aggressive tradition in this country of Catholic radicalism in politics and of social activism that was sometimes directly political and sometimes not.

FAITH, SEX, MYSTERY *Social Activism → sometimes political*

All of this had most of its intellectual roots in Catholic social thinking at the end of the nineteenth century in France and its political ones partly in the Catholic sector of anarcho-syndicalism in Spain and partly in socialist activity everywhere. The two most influential documents of an official kind, I would later learn, were the papal encyclicals *De Rerum Novarum* (*Of New Things*) of Leo XIII in 1891 and *Quadragesimo Anno* (*After Forty Years*) of Pius XII in 1931.

Though anything but radical by present standards, or even by secular ones of their times, these encyclicals, and the entire history of Catholic concern for labor and the poor, astonished me by having existed at all. One of the main barriers to my joining the Church after I'd come to accept its theology and spiritual teachings had been just that illiberalism with which I'd identified it from the period of Father Coughlin. I saw it as at best indifferent to social and political injustice and oppression and, at worst, frankly aligned with the most reactionary and even fascist forces everywhere.

I thought I understood the constituents of this behavior, which struck me as combining the legendary properties of the ostrich and the wolf. I saw it as springing from a number of motives, some of them base—a clinging to power and privilege, a nostalgia for the moral absolutes of the Inquisition, together with the power to enforce them—and some more elevated, at least in theory: they were defending themselves against secularism and the modern corrosive mind, against what they saw as a crumbling sense of eternity. The Church could be aggressive in this regard, as in its swift embrace of Franco at the outset of the Spanish Civil War, or it could simply wait there, obdurate, ungenerous, the castle of belief with its wide moat and every parapet bristling with defenses.

And now in the first months of my life as a member of this

141

Church that had for so long seemed to me without social conscience or compassion I was discovering another side. Or rather, since you couldn't call it a whole "side," I was learning that Catholicism was not quite so monolithic as outsiders thought, in questions of politics and social attitudes, that is. And even in matters of doctrine and practice I would soon come to see that things weren't quite so fixed and unchallengeable as I had believed.

My education was piecemeal and was more a matter of simply encountering people and ideas in the course of my work for the magazine than of any ardent self-instruction; I didn't have a "learning experience." In no particular order that I can recall I became familiar with Dorothy Day and *The Catholic Worker*, both the movement and its newspaper, learned about the worker-priests in France, Brother Pierre, strange saints of the Brazilian slums. I heard about and even met a few tough, salty Irish-American priests who for years had been working on behalf of labor unions and minorities and whose churches served as havens from the medievalism of so much official Catholic thinking. And I discovered *Commonweal* (which I was to begin writing for a few years later).

This magazine, an unofficial publication in that it was edited by laymen and had no affiliation with any diocese or order, was regarded with much suspicion by conservative Catholics (that "so-called" Catholic magazine was something I heard more than once). It was certainly no further left than the Democratic party of the time—these were the years of Adlai Stevenson—but it had been the only Catholic journal to support the Republic against Franco in the Spanish Civil War, as well as being among the very few to denounce Joe McCarthy.

The social activism of the Catholic left, especially the concern for the poor and abused, wasn't necessarily accompanied by political radicalism, which in any case was a relative matter at the time; the term "liberation theology" hadn't yet been coined, for no one had thought to align aspects of Marxism with religious belief. I found to my surprise that such social concern could coexist with conservative politics or none at all.

I remember a tiny magazine called *Integrity*, which was edited by a woman named Dorothy Dohen and for which I wrote a couple of pieces after I'd been at *Jubilee* for a while. As its name suggested, *Integrity* stood for intellectual and spiritual honesty and was marked by a fierce moralism and an impatience with Catholic xenophobia, but as far as I could tell its candor and, it may be, self-righteousness, weren't engaged with any specific politics. Nor did *Jubilee* itself take political stands. Both magazines could have been best described as having purveyed humanism within a Catholic framework, and this kind of humanism, the world regarded under the softer lights of the Gospels, was characteristic of the entire milieu I now inhabited.

This is why the term "Catholic Left" is misleading; it implies political passions and commitments and, as I say, they weren't always present. But the Gospels were, especially their injunction to help the poor and weak. That, for example, most of the people I knew at the time were poor themselves wasn't simply due to the marginally remunerative kinds of work they did but, I knew, was at least in some cases a matter of choice.

What impressed me most, and startled me too, was that many of them seemed (always seemed! I wish I could say with Hamlet, "I know not seems," but how could I get behind so many appearances?) to be more than comfortable with the idea of the Mystical Body, that doctrine which had given me so much difficulty. I remember a quiet lovely woman named Rita Joseph at *Jubilee*. Once when I was depressed over something she talked to me about the Mystical Body, how I was a member of it now and could rely on it for strength and succor.

The sense I got from her and others was that it was a principle of shared suffering as well as of shared grace, and I was sure this was the right way to look at it. But this meant that you were obligated to try to lighten the overload of pain wherever you found it, by assuming your share of the responsibility for God's bad arithmetic.

I remember being intellectually troubled for a time by the apparent contradiction between the idea of the religious life as entailing necessary suffering and the command to try to relieve it in your fellowmen, but it didn't take me long to see that these were very different orders of pain. To suffer from finiteness, estrangement from divinity, the consequences of your own evil, or even to be the victim of chance, is inevitable and a potential source of growth. But to suffer under human injustice and cruelty, to be injured by others in the body and insulted in the spirit, particularly to be the object of execrations based on such arbitrary judgments as race, is for all but the rarest of souls a bitter, useless fate.

I haven't meant to suggest that the magazine was staffed entirely by people aflame with altruism (a masthead of angels!) but only that the ruling atmosphere, the "official" one you might say, was a spirit of democratic ardor. Under the title *Jubilee* on the cover were the words "a magazine of the Church and her people"; the implication was of an equality between the institution and its members, a mild enough assertion, it might be thought, but at the time it gave *Jubilee* an air of being rather radical.

The magazine had been conceived by and started up a year or so before I came there by Rice and Robert Lax, who had been close friends of Thomas Merton at Columbia in the late thirties; Rice in fact had been Merton's godfather when he became a Catholic. Lax, a slightly older man, had been a convert too, from Judaism (Rice was from a solid Irish-Catholic family in Brooklyn). Though I would come to know him fairly well, I never learned anything about his background or the circumstances of his conversion, nor did we ever talk about being Jewish. Lax was, and is, a poet, a very good one some people have thought, although I found his minimalistic, sometimes algebraically mystical ruminations a little less than nourishing.

He was tall and thin, with large teeth and a long, bony horseface that had its own rough beauty, and he walked in a loose-jointed, hurrying manner, perpetually leaning over as though in search of something valuable that might be on the ground. Though he could be dour at times, he could also be extraordinarily funny, with a Jewish, almost Talmudic, flavor to his wit, heavily involved as it was with self-mockery and verbal capers. (I remember a postcard he once sent me that bore only these words in elegant script: "Where There's an Oy, There's a Vey.")

Probably the best way to describe him would be as a "secular monk." He was an extreme ascetic, completely uninterested, as far as I could tell, in material things: food, clothing, all comforts and, there could be no doubt about it, sex. An artist, he even seemed uninterested in art, or rather his aesthetic ideas and tastes were on such a lofty, refined level, and were so entwined with religious considerations, that no contemporary works seemed to please him. I was greatly taken by him, even a little in awe, but because of this harsh and spiritually rarefied attitude toward artistic creation, a worm of doubt about him would wriggle in my head on certain occasions.

One of these stands out in my memory. In the summer of 1954 I saw Beckett's *Waiting for Godot* during its first brief

Anti-intellectualism

run in New York. Pierced by it, wholly enamored, I rushed to tell others, in particular Lax, to whom, I thought, Beckett's extreme spareness and marvelously laconic, grave wit would be especially appealing. He cut off my effusions with a rabbinical dismissal. "I've read it," he said, "and it's nothing but cleverness." Then he went on in some such words as these: "There's no sense of God in it, is there? So it's just a fashionable piece of existential despair." I tried to understand. Out of my sense of the "proper" hierarchy of values I even tried to grant his objection. But I didn't come close to being able to do it. Beckett's play remained for me the supreme work of imagination of our time and was no threat to God, and from then on my esteem for Lax was never quite as high as it had been.

As an aspect of his mystical bent Lax was greatly interested in Eastern religions, from Greek Orthodoxy to Buddhism, and, as my friend and editor, Alice Mayhew, has suggested to me, Merton's later turn to the East, as well as his scarcely hidden contempt for the world, must have owed something to Lax's influence. Certainly he influenced *Jubilee*, which ran a surprising number of articles on Greek and Russian Orthodoxy and on asceticism as an exemplary way of life.

Because Lax drifted in and out of the office, sometimes taking off for months at a time (he would usually go to a mountaintop monastery in Greece, from where he would send cryptic postcards and occasional articles; his title was "roving editor"), *Jubilee* was in most respects very much Ed Rice's baby. He had been a photo editor at *Look*, and his fine visual sense and typographical skills underlay *Jubilee*'s attractive, often sumptuous, appearance. In matters of substance he was chiefly interested in the Liturgy and in Catholic social and educational reform, all of which concerns were reflected in the magazine, but though he had no apparent in-

terest in literature or in any art besides the graphic ones, he
encouraged, or at least allowed, staff members like myself,
Oona Burke and, after I'd left, Wilfrid Sheed, to write on
books, films, theater and so on.

An aloof, unemotional man, Rice was difficult to know
and at times hard to work for; I remember telling him once
that if a boss couldn't pay his workers much money then he
ought to give them love, but the truth was he did neither.
Yet in spite of this, morale at the magazine during my years
there was amazingly high.

When I came *Jubilee* was operating on a shoestring, really
on everyone's will and verve, and it would continue to
struggle until it went under eight or nine years later. The
offices on Park Avenue South had been carved out of a loft
that had previously housed a necktie factory, and despite
every effort to make it more attractive, the place retained
some of its original sweatshop shabbiness, although far from
resenting it we all thought of our working conditions as a
proof of our seriousness and sacrificial dedication, which
helped us put up with the bitterly low pay too.

I remember being excited by the sense of purpose I found
at the magazine, by the asceticism nearly everyone preached
and more or less practiced. I thought of it all as one of those
states of enthusiasm for cleansing or transforming action
such as I had been swept up into before, when as a youth I'd
been on the fringes of various Marxist or quasi-Marxist or
simply pacifist or otherwise humanitarian groups.

As I bring it back to mind, the morale of those groups resembled that of *Jubilee* and of the wider Catholic circle I'd
moved into much more than it did the spirit of the sixties
and seventies. The main difference was that in the earlier period you didn't give much thought to extensive changes in
what is now so barbarously called "life-style," except that
you wanted everything to be simpler, less materialistic. You

FAITH

inhabited the world pretty much the way everyone of your class or caste did, standing at some point along the bounded spectrum of taste, appetite and social relations. But within that you worked for a new efficacy of spirit as it moved through, hovered over, was denied or traduced by "reality," or reinvigorated it.

Although, immersed as I was in the same sort of consciousness as they, I didn't see it at the time, there was something almost painfully touching about the trust most of the people at *Jubilee*, as well as many other Catholics I knew then, seemed to have in the Church as an (eventual) agency of moral and social change. They had faith in the Faith, so to speak; they were convinced, or acted as if they were, that Catholicism, reanimated, purified and restored to its original force and generosity, would in time bring about a rule of love, a reign of peace.

I think suddenly of a line from Federico García Lorca's *Poet in New York:* "The advent of the reign of the ear of corn." A secular image, one might object, an image of natural fecundity. True, but it shares a millennial aspect with the socioreligious atmosphere I was discovering. In the Liturgy "advent" means more than simply one arrival among others; it refers to the coming birth of Christ, its imminence. With that as your model, and if you held fast and worked without getting discouraged and prayed keenly, there would surely come about a ripeness of spirit, a flowering of justice.

And so they worked harder in their magazine (mine too now) at what I would call internal evangelism than at the usual kind, directing their efforts not so much at nonbelievers or people of the "wrong" belief as at the members and institutions of the Faith itself. To be sure, *Jubilee* had a desire, which for obvious reasons I ardently shared, to present a better face of the Church to people outside, to educated Jews and Protestants in particular, but nothing like proselytizing went on in the magazine's pages.

The word we wanted to spread already lay within the Word and was aimed mostly at those of our fellow Catholics (how strange it felt for me to use such a phrase!) whom we considered, or at least told ourselves, were not so much benighted as misinformed. The thing to do, we told them, straightforwardly or more often with sly propagandistic strategies, was relax, relent, open yourselves, be amorous at the sight of change; you must, we said in effect, stop feeling threatened by the way the world keeps adding to itself, complicating and shifting its arrangements. The real enemy was stasis, the arm flung across the eyes to keep out the altered view.

Perhaps the most delicate and affecting strain of naïveté in all this was the implicit address we were making to, the reformation we were urging on, the functionaries and powers of the Church: priests, monks, bishops, the Vatican and the Pope himself. I say "implicit" because unlike what's true today you couldn't at that time take direct public exception to the Church's ordinances or decrees; you couldn't challenge its commands in the spiritual realm or, in a more ambiguous area, publicly condemn the moral or social attitudes of its leaders. (Although nothing prevented us from taking potshots at them among ourselves; we would quickly circulate the latest Cardinal Spellman joke.) The Church had been fashioned out of obedience and was a school for it and so, squirming, inventive, you tried to get round the letter of the law through both innocence and guile.

What you did was set up something resembling a counterculture to the prevailing one, but with almost nothing of defiance in it. You appealed to some better nature within the Catholic community, gave it hints (a photoessay about a nun who worked among the Untouchables in India, approving articles on radical, "universal" Catholic thinkers like Teilhard de Chardin), cajoled it and, I suppose it's true to say, implicitly tried to shame it back to the original injunctions to love one's neighbor and all God's handiwork, not selections from among that. A few years later the coming to the Papacy of John XXIII would seem to many people the miracle they'd been soliciting, but at the time I'm writing about Pius XII still reigned.

I sit here and remember: qualities of the mind, what the air was like. Something that comes back to me again is that we were all so naive. It wasn't that we had the crystalline, childlike, unconditioned ardor of certain saints I knew about, but that we weren't able to understand just how complex, knotty and devious the human world really is. This is of course true of all revolutionary or even reforming fervor and is one thing Camus meant when he wrote that all revolutionaries end up by becoming either tyrants or heretics.

Along with the trust we all had in the Church's potential humanization, or maybe as an aspect of it, almost all the Catholics I knew during this period had an unspoken yearning to be *part of the world*, not to be left out of it. The mood was very much the opposite of that of the early Christians and of that condition of defensive religiosity in which so many Catholics and fundamentalist Protestants—as well as some stringently orthodox Jews and Moslems for that matter—are held today, a state of morale in which hatred and contempt for "Godless" society mingles with extreme fear of it.

Well, we *were* part of the world, if not as much as we would have liked to be in ideas, imaginative or intellectual accomplishments and the like, then surely in the struggle we shared with nonbelievers in moral and psychic realms. Along with our social consciences, our actual and maybe as often theoretical love of the poor and outcast, our love of God for that matter, we could have all sorts of defects of character and personality, some of these peculiar to a certain type of humanitarian zealot. We could be disfigured by humorlessness, by crimped passions in the natural order, a narrow general outlook. We could deny our revulsion from the injured and the squalid, and be blind to the envy we must have felt at times toward those who were spiritually more advanced than ourselves.

How could it have been otherwise? I remember how hard a time I had liking some of the people I worked among and was thrown together with at the time (some of them undoubtedly disliked me) and how, feeling guilty about that, I tried to love them instead. I had learned about that disinterested, "higher" modality called *agape*, and I tried to shape my attitudes under its light. But I wasn't very successful at it; trivial dislikes—of a hairstyle, a way of speaking, a bad complexion—kept breaking in. I remember a man who worked for a while at *Jubilee* whose obnoxious laugh—explosive, earsplitting, instigated by occasions that were sometimes funny but more often not—would incite in me a loathing so intense that I had to take it to Confession as a sin against charity.

As a group were we better or worse than the people "outside"? At least the visible signs of egotism were muted. More than that, a few of the Catholics I met at this time, both priests and laymen, struck me as being close to saintly, as I had thought Father Walsh was. Yet I was never sure if their goodness could be attributed to their faith—would they have been that way without it?—or was a natural pos-

RICHARD GILMAN

session, a gift which Catholicism in its fundamental moral teachings simply confirmed or to which it gave a protective structure.

It's a commonplace to say that nonreligious people can be morally splendid and, conversely, that to be religious is far from guaranteeing kindness and even further from ensuring self-sacrifice. For a great many persons religion indeed serves, in most cases unconsciously, as a mask for selfishness, a form of self-aggrandizement under the guise of humility. So self-evident is this that I have to explain why I bring it up here.

At the time I'm writing about I understood that Catholicism couldn't be morally efficacious at every moment, yet I childishly wanted it to be. I wanted it to work on the model of a wonder drug or, if that was too farfetched, of the red corpuscles in the body's fight against disease, tirelessly attacking the infection, disarming and obliterating the enemy and so allowing health to shine through. I wanted faith to be a means of healing character defects, petty or huge, so that all of us would be more humane. And I wanted the transformation to *show*.

It was a sign of my immaturity that I should crave these things, just as it had been one in New Orleans when I had expected the Church to wipe away my depression and meliorate my estrangement. But I was to be forever bumping up against such idle hopes. Part of my education, imperfect as it was to turn out, lay in coming to understand that if religion isn't a cure, neither is it a preventative. We're in the natural world, we have our bodies, which go their way; we have desires, traits of being that sometimes accord with the spirit and sometimes don't.

I knew all that then, abstractly, but for a long time I acted as if I didn't, perpetually surprised by the persistence in me and others of what we call the "old Adam." Wasn't that

Original Sin

supposed to have taken flight the moment the baptismal water touched my forehead? Well, it hadn't, of course, and never would; it would remain in me as a metaphor, a term to describe a continuing struggle.

In the light of all this it wasn't strange that when I first came among Catholics I should have been especially alert to, yet at the same time queasy about knowing, what they did in regard to sex, how they dealt with its dominion and bite. For wasn't that where the old Adam chiefly operated and hadn't my own history piled up annals of carnal engagement, suffering and crisis? I hadn't become a Catholic out of a violent repudiation of the flesh, but now that I was one I felt a need to learn how it was possible to live with carnality under the laws of spirit, how you could manage the juggling act or catch-as-catch-can bout between their often conflicting demands.

Nobody was going to teach me directly. I was much too inhibited to talk about sex with my new Catholic friends and acquaintances, who, for their part, weren't given to bringing the subject up. So I found myself limited to observing them, to be sure obliquely, semiconsciously, and feeling a little guilty about it, as though I were an especially sly sort of Peeping Tom in their midst. In the end I drew up a rough typology, or I do it now in retrospect.

As was to be expected there were some people from whom I couldn't take any readings, since they offered no clues, and there were others about whom a great deal could be known, had I chosen or been able to recognize it. Liz Sullivan and Joan Paul, for example, the women who owned the Paraclete bookshop, were almost surely a lesbian couple, but I never allowed the knowledge to sink in, most likely because I wouldn't have known what to do with it.

(From what I learned later Joan was in love with Liz while she, as Joan remarked after her death, had spent her passion searching for the "perfect liturgy." Not long after Liz died Joan was stabbed to death by her roommate.)

At the time I shared the prevailing view of homosexuality as something dark and unnatural, and it's probable that I didn't want to acknowledge it in these friends because that would have meant having to deal with its implications for their Catholicism. And since for all my avowed desire to learn, I didn't want to learn about anything that might undermine my hope that the Church would give me some protection against the "perverse" side of my own nature, I stayed blind to what must have been obvious to everyone else.

The people I *could* furtively study fell, rather too neatly I now think, into three main groups. To begin with there were those, usually though not always married, for whom nothing seemed amiss or problematic; a few couples I knew indeed gave off a strong feeling of well-being, suggesting an easy and supple movement between transcendence and the body. Then there were the sexual ascetics, dogged, determined ones or, in some cases, untroubled, perched comfortably on a pillar of renunciation in the mind. Lax, for instance, didn't strike me as suffering under his abjuration of carnality or as fighting anything off.

Finally there were some whom I saw as washed out and exhausted. I thought of them as victims of their own childhood and youth, their training, during which they had been morosely drilled in the proposition that sex was at best only *acceptable*, within narrow limits at that. And now as adults they might have the abstract conviction that sex was better than this, that it could bring replenishment and joy, but naturally they couldn't act on this humanist belief, much less on their desire.

(The only worse Catholic utterance on the subject I know of than Saint Paul's "It is better to marry than to burn" is

Pascal's "[Marriage] is the lowest of the conditions of Christianity, vile and prejudicial in the eyes of God." It's a good thing I didn't come upon this until long after I had left the Church.)

Nearly all my unmarried friends and colleagues lived celibately, as far as I knew (but what could I really know?) and did it either with apparent sangfroid, unmarked by any sign of strain, or, as in the cases of the sufferers I mentioned before, in a kind of etiolated condition, blanched in an almost visible way by unacknowledged or suppressed erotic cravings. Sometimes their defenses collapsed under the pressure of the blood and nerves. I think of something that happened when I had been at *Jubilee* for a couple of years, an event whose implications for me went far beyond the immediate social or psychological facts of the matter.

A young woman of twenty-eight or -nine, a secretary and clerk in the office, was, as we all knew, in love with a somewhat older man, a charming and irresponsible fellow, or so she had led us to believe, who, moreover, was already married and wasn't a Catholic. She had been growing increasingly agitated as, apparently, their affair moved toward some crisis whose nature we could only speculate on, all of us knowing that the situation was furnished with complicated possibilities of disaster.

I arrived at the office a little late one morning to find everyone sitting together or walking about in agitation and gloom. Sometime during the night the woman had fallen to her death from the terrace of her boyfriend's pied-à-terre on a high floor in some apartment complex, Peter Cooper Village, I think it was. As Catholics it was hard for us to believe that she might have jumped, or at any rate to admit that we suspected it, so we kept telling each other that it must have been an accident, although something greatly overwrought and despairing must have led up to that and most of us agreed that the boyfriend had probably played a sinister role in the matter.

The funeral was in Jersey City, where the woman's family lived, and we all went out to it in several cars. It was a late winter day, gray, drizzling, chilly, made all the more depressing by the woebegone seediness of the place after that dismal drive from Manhattan. In the funeral parlor (or was it the family's home? I can't remember) the woman lay in an open coffin and I was horrified to see that some sort of repairs had been done on her head, which must have been crushed in the fall, for her skull was noticeably smaller than it had been in life, lopsided and *artificial*. Throughout the lugubrious conversation and embarrassed condolences to the family, who stood grieving and bewildered, and later during the funeral Mass for the Dead at some hideous brown pile of a Catholic church, we all continued to act on the assumption that her death had been an accident, but without any evidence I felt more and more certain that this wasn't true.

We drove back to the city in the late darkening afternoon, five or six of us in the car, everyone silent, everyone in need of a drink, which we got at the first bar we could find after we left the tunnel. We sat there glumly, making small talk, none of us willing to say what we were really thinking. Then we reluctantly broke up, moving out of the circle of one another's reassuring presence, and I went off to the place I was staying for a few days, the Upper East Side apartment of my friend Luna Tarlo, who was out of town at the moment.

When I got there I rode up in the elevator, unlocked the door to the apartment, walked into the foyer, turned on the light, took off my raincoat and was all at once assailed by a spasm of terror. The dead woman was in the apartment, or rather she was in there dead but also at the same time "alive." I could "see" her; she was moving about in the next room or the one beyond that, in the pink, high-collared dress she had worn in her coffin, with the same sad, crushed and reconstituted head. There was a peculiar smile on her face, which changed, as I stood there paralyzed, to a grimace of reproach, but directed against whom?

Fighting my panic I forced myself to go into the living room and then through all the other rooms, turning on all the lights, the TV, several radios, a record player, in an attempt to fill the big apartment with noise and distraction. But it was as though she were keeping just ahead of me, moving from room to room, and would at any moment turn back to make her presence known. She would come to me and embrace me, I thought, press my cheek to her ruined one; I would feel compelled to stroke her freezing blond hair and then she would softly whisper some harrowing question in my ear. I would have her deadness in my arms. She would lead me off to the bedroom . . .

I remember doing the most clichéd things to try to drive away the apparition: shaking my head violently, pressing my fist into my mouth. Finally I ran to the bar and fixed myself a stiff Scotch and then another, but they did nothing to dispel the horror. So at last I floundered toward the foyer, walking as though in a swamp, having to will every step, got my coat and rushed into the elevator and out into Lexington Avenue, leaving all the lights on in the haunted apartment.

As I thought about it afterward this dreadful hallucinatory experience seemed to be somehow in the line of the "supernatural" visitations that had figured so prominently in my movement toward the Church. Yet on the face of it those others had been very different. The earlier ones had been anything but terrifying or dismaying, except in the sense that one is likely to quail before such revelations that a divine realm exists. Then why had this one been so appalling and where had it come from? Was the dead woman a hallucination in the clinical sense?

I remembered Hamlet's crucial problem near the beginning of the play: to decide whether his father's ghost is an emanation from "above" or "below," from Heaven or Hell. In my case I had to ask myself whether what had happened was an irruption from my psyche, the neurotic part of it at that, and therefore the "below" of the matter, or something arranged from on high. I've never been able to decide; how could I? But what I do know is that the occurrence has remained profoundly implicated in the thoughts I never stop having about my own potential death and that it took place to instruct me in the true, dangerous relations between body and spirit and so between physical and moral being.

I had never before "seen" or felt the presence of a ghost, or perhaps zombie would be more accurate in this instance. I'd always thought horror films silly, especially the genre that features the "living dead." Then why should it have happened that for the first and only time in my life, during a period when I was a firm believer in Catholicism, which I thought of as the enemy of all superstition, a bulwark against the occult, I came upon or dreamed such a thing? The day and the circumstances played their parts, no doubt; so dismal a weather, so unnerving and calamitous an occasion. But they could only have provided the opportunity or ground for what had happened, not the cause.

Whatever was behind it I knew that the apparition had spoken to me, in its melancholy unrest, about mortality; it had told me, for one thing, that life was separated from death by only the thinnest line and that sometimes they spilled over into one another, in the mind of course, which is the only place where they can mingle. From then on I knew that I couldn't live, as a believer or not, with any clean and absolute division between being and not-being: I'm here now, then I'm *there*. Though of course like everyone else I've tried to handle it that way.

There was something else. I brushed off the sexual implications at the time, or rather I fled from them, but they caught up. Whatever the facts of her fatal plunge the woman had died from within the disaster area that's so often created by the erotic in collision with "higher" values. I was convinced that her despair had been brought on by a struggle between faith and desire, something I thought I knew about. Or if she hadn't fully believed, or had even lost her religion, then the battle had been between desire and the *habit* of faith, its unconscious residual promptings of her behavior.

I don't know what her spiritual condition was, whether she was in a state of grace or in despair, and it isn't the point. The two dominions clashed in her and go on doing it in all of us: the transcendent and the immediate, faith, which has always to be offered to the invisible, and human craving for bodies, for bodily blessings.

It was a story of this kind that I later decided she would have whispered to me, at once a cautionary tale, a plea for understanding and a lament. And the ghastly seduction I had imagined would then have been her—its—way of showing me that I couldn't stand apart, that religion wasn't a reliable means of erotic sublimation, as I had been trying to make it be, that the mysteries were deeper than I knew and that, in my yearning toward "perfection," my (probably) Manichaean view of body and spirit, I wasn't any better than she and probably worse. And I wasn't any safer.

This has brought me far ahead of my story, so I must go back. There wasn't any sort of job for me at the magazine, Ed Rice told me the first time I saw him, though I was welcome to hang around. But after a few days, on the strength of the bookstore owners' recommendation, my evident eagerness and my pinched situation, he managed to come up with something.

Would I be willing to go out and try to sell the magazine door to door? By this he meant calling at Catholic rectories, schools and libraries, where they had been having a hard time getting a foothold. And no wonder. For all that Manhattan was a center of left-wing Catholic activity (Chicago was even more so at the time) this was a thoroughly unofficial and fringe phenomenon, frowned on, deplored or completely ignored by the great majority of those involved in the institutional Church.

My first reaction to the proposal was neither dismay nor ready assent, but a doubtfulness that rested as much on my improbable talent for salesmanship as on considerations of the lowly nature of the job. (My salary was to be thirty dollars a week; they didn't dare ask me to do it on commission!) But I wasn't in any position to refuse. So I swallowed the clot of pride that had automatically risen in me and quickly convinced myself that my purported charm and real loquacity were splendid assets for a salesman. A few days later, armed with copies of the magazine, order forms and street maps, and having been briefed in the best way to deal with the indifference or hostility I was surely going to encounter, I set out.

Nothing could have prepared me for what happened. In the first place, my lack of success was nearly unbroken. During the three weeks or so I kept at it, working from various lists and covering the island from Harlem to City Hall, I managed to place only a few small orders for the magazine racks of some churches and sell subscriptions to a couple of libraries and the rare "progressive" priest, usually a younger man, I came upon.

But for the most part it was like trying to talk to Eskimos. The typical object of my spiel turned out to be an elderly Irish or Italian pastor, the former most often heavyset and gruff of speech, impatient or bellicose in manner, the latter usually bespectacled, distracted and in possession of an English that was no doubt adequate for routine sacerdotal dealings with his flock but for not much else (had all these priests recently been imported from Italy to make up some shortage?) and who in any case, like his Irish counterpart, seemed to have a social vision bounded by bingo games and the smooth operation of street festivals or, at best, visit-the-sick programs. Or else I met that species of nun or laywoman with thin lips and a steely glance who seemed, in astonishing obedience to the stereotype, to be in charge of almost all Catholic school libraries. And on all these people my charm made no visible impression and my way with words, on the few occasions when I was given time to display it, was completely unpersuasive.

It took me a long time to understand or rather to acknowledge how I really felt during those strange weeks. To begin with, I said that I had swallowed my pride and this was true, initially. But I could never manage to keep it all the way down and had to stay alert to the possibility of its reasserting itself at any moment. The danger then would be that I might suddenly find myself responding to some florid-faced monsignor's diatribe against liberalism or praise of McCarthy (it was 1954, remember) by telling him to fuck off.

Yet it wasn't so much the substance of these encounters that troubled me, the social or political disagreement or worse, as the raw fact that I was doing this. I was putting myself in the presence, the momentary power you could say, of people with whom I had nothing in common, since the only connection, the faith we ostensibly shared, seemed in these circumstances to divide rather than unite us. More than that, I had contempt for most of them, no matter how hard I tried to suppress it.

It wasn't an abstract contempt, the result of an *a priori* judgment, say, or if that entered into it it did so unconsciously. Again my naïveté was pulling me by the ear. Why should I have been so surprised by the people I met on these rounds? Didn't I know that most Catholics, most people, were full of prejudices and that some of them were bigots? They had no compassion, I thought, but what was my own like, my willed loving-kindness and theoretical sense of responsibility? And wasn't I a self-righteous interloper? Who was I, a Catholic for three months, to presume to show these people how to be better Christians and what was I doing in offering them a "truer" version of the Faith? But I see all this only now.

The contempt I felt for some of them was a response to the way they looked—a dirty cassock, a chomped cigar, the pallor of nuns—and even more to the impression they gave, when they weren't grubby or seedy or unhealthy-looking, of a peculiar abstraction. There was a metallic quality about many of them, something thin-blooded and, for whatever reason, slightly embittered. They seemed to hang on the edge of surliness, with quick tempers, barely hidden resentments. Some of them made me think of civil servants stuck in unpromising jobs or bus drivers who dislike their routes.

I wasn't being fair, I can see that now. I was flaying them with the pitiless idealism of the convert who holds up higher standards than can ever be met. I summon up some images of them and can see now how harried they were, how beset. For along with the universal urban tensions they had to contend with there were those that came from the very nature of their vocations and roles. And were they personally responsible for their surroundings, the gloom and sterility of rectories or the military look of Catholic schools? But I blamed them anyway.

What made my distress worse was that I was trying to *sell* them something, with all that this meant of artificial, tactical deference, politeness and goodwill. I was a salesman, a role which out of my imprecise and doubtless naive adversary position toward American social reality I had always considered to be low, degrading, a loss of self. I had a "line," patter, a *brisk opening*, and in a fundamental way it didn't seem to matter that I also had a cause, that I believed, with a fair amount of ardor, in my "product."

Yet only a year or two earlier I had gone out to knock on doors with a Citizens for Stevenson kit under my arm and had tried to convince potential voters that he and not Eisenhower was the true savior. And I hadn't been nearly so embarrassed or uncomfortable as I felt now. I had been selling something then, hadn't I? Had my faith in politics and Adlai Stevenson been deeper and more passionate than my Catholicism was now? That was hardly likely.

I must try to sort it all out. The fact was that I felt humiliated all through this time, abashed at what I was doing, and I could only keep going by alternately reminding myself of the justice and importance of what I represented and, in a more practical vein, telling myself that if I could see it through the editors would be impressed enough to offer me something more satisfying and productive to do.

From the moment I put my finger on the first buzzer, at a rectory on the Upper East Side, I think it was, I was in a perpetual state of disorientation. The contrast with my "selling" of Adlai Stevenson suddenly becomes clear. I'd done that after hours, as a hobby, you might say, a gesture of freedom; it wasn't my job. But now if someone were to ask me what I *did* in life I would have had to answer "I sell magazine subscriptions door to door." I suppose my state of mind resembled that of a sensitive and un-company-minded Fuller Brush man or a Ph.D. forced by hard times to an assembly line.

I was oppressed by a sense of total indistinctness. I felt like a cog, a replaceable part or— no, that's not quite it. It was more that I couldn't recognize in what I was doing the dream I'd had of myself, that vision of keen specificity and bold originality which I'd associated with being a writer and which I'd been suppressing for some time. But now it began to torment me and it was only part of what did.

The turmoil and self-division I was undergoing rose from a terrific shock of estrangement, the sundering from my past which this peddling of magazines made clear. I was a Catholic now (how often have I repeated those words in these pages, as though I have to make sure that I keep rhythmically announcing the staggering difference it made in my life!). But up to now I had ridden with the change in the safety of my skull, cherishing my secret lofty move, fighting off momentary weakness, as in New Orleans, and being protected by this commitment of my spirit from the disorderly, irreverent and treacherous claims of actuality.

Earlier I spoke of having felt "out of" the world after my baptism, impelled by supernatural forces and designs and sustained by altered ambitions, chief among them an aspiration toward spiritual or inner perfection instead of toward making my way in the world. I spoke of feeling relieved of competitiveness, the constant need to make comparisons between myself and others.

Now I was back in the world, right down in it, talking about subscription rates and discounts for bulk orders, defining myself by the success or failure of each particular sales pitch while trying all the time to remind myself of the beauty of abnegation and the virtue of my little martyrdom. The worst thing was having to, or at least finding that I did, measure myself against others, aware of every blatant or subtle difference in behavior, personality and mind. I was back in a psychological and social realm after having thought I could pitch myself above them.

As a result of all this, although I was only fitfully conscious of it at the time, my sense of being Jewish returned during these weeks, and with it that peculiar feeling, so familiar to Jews—at any rate of my generation and earlier—of being at the same time vulnerable, in a way "guilty," and superior. The superiority seldom has anything to do with religious belief. Oh, I know there are some Jews—rabbis, Talmudic scholars, ardent lay people here and there—who consider Judaism to be the best of all religions, to be in fact religion itself. But nearly all the Jews I've known, beginning with my own family and on into the society, haven't thought that way at all. Insofar as they practice their faith they do it out of an amalgam of habit, tribal loyalty, ethnic solidarity, a bit of defiance perhaps, but almost never with a theological arrogance or even assurance. In my experience Judaism is more a principle of identity than an active faith, for all the recent movements of Jewish "renewal."

In my case, moreover, I had accepted Catholicism just because I considered it superior as a religion to Judaism or any other creed I knew about. I thought it fuller, further-going, more demanding, *truer*. So the superiority I felt as a Jew didn't have anything to do with religious belief, quite the opposite. It was a secular emotion, if I can describe it that way, only partly rational and otherwise instinctive, something in the blood and racial memory and in the memory of my own childhood, when, surely with no notion of theology or even of what as a Jew I was supposed to believe, I felt I was better than the Italians, Poles and Irish people, the Christians, I knew or saw.

When in the circumstances I've been describing my Jew-

ishness revived, it reasserted a principle of identity, uniqueness, that was intimately connected to my esteem for
intellect and creativity—ours, Jews'—and that had been ob-
cured or given an otherworldly cast by my new faith. When
I was baptized I had thought myself unique for a time, it's
true, since I'd accomplished what I considered a mighty
leap beyond the power of others to make. But this was a secret between me and God; now I felt the pressure of other
judgments, other standards, ones that were public, worldly,
and by which I was at least temporarily found wanting.

To live in the spirit seemed to mean the loss of a distinctive sense of self in society, of any sense of self at all, for that
matter. It meant you had to live with invisible attributes,
unmarketable "skills." Or so it appeared to me as I made my
salesman's rounds. I would recover from this disconsolateness, or get round it, after the editors decided to end my stint
in the streets and found other work for me in the office. But
it never wholly left me and was to flare up again much more
strongly after a time.

I've been talking about a renewed sense of Jewishness and
I realize that I haven't yet spoken of my family in regard to
my having become a Catholic. The truth is that I kept it
from them and that there was never a time when I thought
of telling them. I hadn't even revealed to them anything
about my growing interest in religion during the months
leading up to my baptism and after that I saw every reason
to stay silent.

My parents were perfunctory Jews. I can't remember
them ever talking to me about religion, which inhabited our
household in the form of a number of mechanical rituals and
taboos. They went to the synagogue only for the most important holy days in the spring and fall, held an annual seder
and, later, made the customary gestures toward the memory

of their own parents, who had been much more orthodox and pious than they. But, I knew, psychologically they were Jewish to the core. And if even I had thought of Christians as the enemy in my childhood, how much more deep-seated must this fear have been in them?

Fear, and revulsion as well. I knew that among Jews there was a practice of regarding someone who becomes a Christian as "dead," so that one then sits shivah over that person the way it's done for the physically deceased. I didn't think my parents would go that far but I could see my mother wailing at the news, tearing her hair or, most likely, falling over in a dead faint, and my father hurling curses at my head. And I could imagine my sister Edith, a quite sophisticated and liberal woman, to whom I was very close, looking at me in stricken incomprehension.

There hadn't been anything defiant in my conversion, quite the contrary. It hadn't been aimed at my family or my past, which meant that I didn't have any itch to throw it at them as a repudiation of their way of life, in the manner of a sixties flower-child, say, or a present-day Hare Krishnan. And so, since I couldn't expect them to begin to understand why I had done it, I saw no point in inflicting such dumb pain on them. Therefore they never knew, although there were times when it became clear to me that they suspected. But they couldn't bring themselves to take it out into the open and I lulled them by explaining that the Catholic magazines I worked for, *Jubilee* and later *Commonweal*, were extremely "progressive" and had a number of non-Catholic contributors, including Jews like me. Beyond that, their relief at my finally having a job was enough to quell every suspicion or doubt.

I'm not sure what I would have done had they asked me about it point-blank, though I suspect I would have lied. This may be a rationalization for cowardice, but I don't think so. Honesty in such matters, or "sincerity," as we fashionably call it now, is an unstable virtue behind which can lurk arrogance or an insane dream of purity. Perhaps I was wrong, but it seemed to me, too, that I needed to guard my conversion against a disclosure that would only have resulted in its being thoroughly misinterpreted, and hence degraded, by my family and most of the people in my past.

So there I was, a semisecret Catholic, though not at most times a furtive one. I had told a few friends, the ones I thought would be neither shocked nor critical, and most of them were indeed sympathetic, if not enthusiastic. But my new faith meant new daily concerns as well as altered values, all of which cut me off from a great part of my previous life, so that for the next few years I moved as an immigrant, so to speak, with Catholicism as my new country and environment and Jewishness as the "Old World." And this meant that my life in New York was different in nearly every respect from what it had been before.

For some months I shared an apartment on York Avenue with a young man, Albert, whom I had met through the bookstore. He was a kind, gentle fellow, extremely pious (he later became a monk) and supportive of my struggle to acclimatize myself in the Faith. His piety had a somewhat desperate edge to it, I realize now, for it was what kept his homosexuality, which I knew about but kept putting out of my mind, from turning into physical acts.

Almost all my friends for the next few years were new and nearly all were Catholic. I forget some of their names and remember others: Lax, Bob Reynolds and Oona Burke from *Jubilee;* Janet Knight, Nicholas Arcomano, Barbara LaRosa, Jill and Jacques Lowe, Ruby Del Archiprete (such a glorious name!). I remember them fondly. At the time I thought of them, of us, as a band of outsiders, connected to one another by the invisible ties Catholicism made as it stood against, more truly beyond, the secular world; but we were also a band within a band, all of us working or simply living near the fringe of the Church, with which most of us were to one degree or another embattled.

We rode our hopes for a redemption that wouldn't exclude others (I think of Simone Weil in this regard), tried to be open and kindly, to be catholic as well as Catholic; the lowercase word—from the Greek for "completely whole"—testifies to a time when the uppercase one denoted the fullest universality mankind had yet reached. And we struggled in our various ways with such moral or psychic difficulties as each of us had, while at the same time, like everyone else, we needed physically just to get along.

One thing most of us did was to indulge or pursue our "advanced" or unparochial tastes. I don't mean to give the impression of a cultic exuberance or to imply that we were full of self-congratulation about how creative and liberated we were. If anything our effort to bring natural opinions and inclinations into line with supernatural commandments was more than a little innocent and made for some (mostly unconscious) strain. For we were living as though the Church and Catholicism could be what we made them, as if they were already transformed or were about to be. And of course nothing like that was true.

Anyway we decorated our apartments and offices with the new liturgical art (Sister Mary Corita was an artist I remember from this time; she had a little of Matisse's knowing innocence, his swoops of color and delighted naive shapes). We went to simple Masses at unpretentious little churches whose pastors' politics or social consciences we admired. And, along with the obligatory rituals, we did things at Christmas and Easter that were "purer," closer, we felt, to what it once must have been like: going to Greek or Russian

Intellect, Sin
Original

Orthodox ceremonies, making special sacrifices for the poor and giving one another gifts that seemed to us modest and appropriate: good bread, candles, books of poetry, well-wrought little mementos of the Faith.

As I look back on it I think that for the most part they weren't people I'd have been likely to choose as friends in my previous life, or they me, but then what besides my conversion could ever have brought us together? As it was, I *fell in with them*, these figures in my new milieu, the way it happens when for whatever reason you move to a new place with changed circumstances: they were the people I was now among. And even as I tried to find in them whatever was closest to the qualities I'd looked for in others before, I responded to and often welcomed some of their differences from the people I had known.

With some exceptions, several people at *Jubilee*, for example, I thought my new friends and associates in those first years not as intellectually complicated as I was, and chided myself for making anything of it. But with some sentimentality I also saw them as morally better. Or no, not quite that. I thought of them as having the advantage over the people I used to know of being conscious victims of Original Sin; they knew that there was a crack or flaw in human nature and so weren't likely to lapse into a dream of being healed through their own efforts (or through "therapy"), nor were they likely to accept society as the chief arbiter of moral truth or see success in this life as exculpation.

With another strain of sentimentality no doubt, I remember being moved by the various psychic or emotional wounds—or at least problems—many of them seemed to have and, up to a point, sharing my own with them. Were their maladies or neuroses more widespread or severe than those of the people in my past? Not at all, but theirs were different or rather were held in a different framework; they kept pressing up against spiritual considerations. And this made for still another form of tacit bonding: we were linked by injury and by the relief that came from not having to hide it from one another or try rationally to account for all of it.

It wasn't that we paraded our scars, nor was there anything victimlike in our behavior. We didn't sit around commiserating or talk much about our psyches. But we were tolerant of each other's turmoil and depressions, we'd give one another tips about modes of prayer designed for special situations in the moral and psychic life (I hadn't any to offer at first) and pray for one another after having been informed about a crisis or a sudden accession of pain. With its pleasures and sorrows it was a true if informal community, the only one I've ever belonged to, and for all that I never felt wholly at ease in it I have many moments when I feel a stab of regret at its loss.

There's something else I haven't yet talked about in regard to my being Jewish. I've spoken of some of the things I felt about it but not of the attitudes of my new friends and the other Catholics I met at this time. Never for a moment did I think that I wasn't Jewish anymore, as though it had all been wiped away by my baptism; nothing had been wiped away by it, although something certainly had been added.

But in nearly every case the Catholics among whom I was living and working went further than I did: they saw my Jewishness as actively continuing, fulfilled by my conversion and in no way canceled by it. But they were thinking of Judaism as a religion, a matter of belief or at least of spiritual inclination, whereas I hadn't for a long time felt any of that, if I ever had.

Naturally they knew as well as I did that my being a Jew ethnically or sociologically (physically too? I mean a quality of the blood, in the bones, not of the hair or nose) wasn't changed in any way by my conversion. I would forever be in that ambiguous condition where one is Jewish no matter what the state of one's belief, that category for which the only ultimate criterion, the only practical one anyway, may be Sartre's dictum that the Jew is the person whom others see as being one.

As I say, my friends knew all about that but most of them wanted, rather romantically I thought, for my "case" to transcend such earthbound, sociopolitical considerations, with their implications of persecution or at the very least unhappiness. They were thinking of the pure spirit and saw what had happened to me as exemplary of one of its movements. In this they very much resembled certain Catholic or Protestant theological and spiritual writers who are abstractly amorous toward Jews. They think of the New Testament as the fulfillment of the Old and so, in their perspective, because the Jews were the people of the Book, singled out by God, and because Jesus, Mary, Joseph and the disciples had all been Jewish and went on being it, Christians were obligated to be grateful to and honor both Jewish people and Judaism itself. I imagine something of this was also true in colonial America among those who named their children Samuel and Abraham, Rachel and Rebecca.

To be sure all this was as remote as it could be from the historical mainstream of Christian attitudes and, more to the point, behavior toward us, and I'm quite aware that the Catholics I was closest to and the writers I was reading were highly unrepresentative. Indeed on the edges of the world I lived in I would occasionally encounter one or another type and degree of anti-Semitism, almost always exhibited in ignorance of my identity and, if the person were apprised of that, as he or she usually was, invariably followed by apologies, lame, embarrassed or, more rarely, full of genuine shock and, as far as I could tell, remorse.

But I can see that for the most part I was insulated from hatred or even dislike of Jews, as for very different reasons I had been in my childhood and youth; if anything, anti-Catholicism was much more of a problem for me now than anti-Semitism had ever been. It's hard for me to believe that I was the only Jewish convert these people knew, but maybe it was so, for they never mentioned any other except for one or two they'd read about, and Bob Lax, who didn't count. Lax was a Jewish convert all right, but he inhabited so delicate and lofty a realm of mysticism and was seemingly so remote from earthly considerations that everyone thought of him as sui generis, beyond classification.

And so I was treated with special kindness, it seemed, more specifically with an amalgam of astonishment and solicitude. The astonishment I knew came from their sense of my having done something that must have been extraordinarily difficult and frightening, and the solicitude rose, I suspected, from their belief that I remained highly vulnerable. Beyond this I would from time to time detect a note of gratitude, such as I described before in the reaction to the news of my conversion which the women at the bookstore had displayed.

As may be imagined all this made me uncomfortable at times, especially when the assumption was clear on someone's part that I'd been a religious Jew for whom Catholicism was the culmination of a persistent search instead of being the place I landed on after a leap from total atheism. At such times I'd feel a little guilty or pained that I'd disappointed the person, who after all was surely well-meaning and had probably cast me as the protagonist of a well-made play, a religious drama in which I moved in act one from the Old Testament, to doubt and quest in act two and finally to the glad tidings of the New Testament at the denouement. "You've gone from Jerusalem to Rome," someone in fact once said to me, admiringly if also rather sententiously. And so, as often as not, I lent myself to the role or at least didn't dispute it.

I haven't meant to imply that I was always fawned over or treated with spectacular deference, yet on a few occasions something like that was indeed true. I think in particular of the two days I once spent at a Carthusian monastery in Vermont, where I was fussed, prayed and marveled over as though without knowing it I myself were the bearer of glad tidings.

Along with the photographer Jacques Lowe I had been sent to the monastery to do a story for *Jubilee*. It was the middle of winter, I remember, and violently cold. We got to the monastery late in the evening and were shown by a lay brother to the place where we were to sleep, a room, in an old wooden building, that contained nothing more than a couple of cots with some rough blankets. There was no light and no heat at all and so, our teeth clacking, our faces—had we been able to see them—surely turning blue, we lay down under the blankets with all our clothes on, including our gloves and overcoats, and slept on and off until dawn.

The brother soon came to show us to a bathroom, where we washed in icy water (we were also brought hot water for shaving), and then took us to breakfast, coffee and dark, home-baked, not very tasty bread, which we ate in a big steamy kitchen where several brown-robed brothers were preparing the day's fare, exceedingly simple, as it turned out. Then he took us to meet the abbot. He was a tall, gaunt, bespectacled man in his fifties wearing the white flannel or woolen cowled robe of the order. He had a crisp, efficient manner and wasted no time in telling us that he and the others were "delighted" and "honored" by the presence among them of, I think he said, "two souls of Jewish origin."

I was puzzled for a moment by his having referred to the "two" of us, until I remembered that one of Jacques's parents had been Jewish—his mother, I believe. But how did the abbot know about our backgrounds? Obviously someone at the magazine must have told him in connection with our visit. But if that were so, what was the point? As I thought about it later I decided that the informant had wished the abbot to treat us with special kindness, or, at least, particular attention, and that our being Jewish, in my case a convert, was at the outside interesting and at the center a source of prayerful appreciation and concern.

Whatever was behind it, for the rest of our stay (until early afternoon of the following day) the abbot and the monks we met made much of us, especially, it seemed, of me, the convert. After meeting the abbot, Lowe went off to take photos of the place, which must have been a farm at one time: a large wooden house, a barnlike building, a wooden chapel and some huts or cabins scattered across the slightly undulating fields now deep under snow. When we were alone the abbot questioned me about my life and interests and then, as though having ascertained to his satisfaction the facts he needed, led me off toward one of the cabins.

As we trudged along a path cut through the snow he told me that the monks lived alone in these huts, praying, reading and, in one case, writing, and met only once a day, for evening prayers; their meals, of the plainest kind, were brought to them by the lay brothers, some of whom, he said, were aspirants to the priesthood while others were content to remain in their humble status for good. He also told me, which I already knew, that a rule of silence prevailed—the Carthusians were even more strict in this regard than the better-known Trappists—there being only a one-hour weekly period during which they could get together and chat. For practical reasons he and the lay brothers could speak as the occasion called for and, with his permission, the monks could talk to visitors like me.

The cabin we were going to looked closer across the sun-bright snow than it actually was, so the abbot had time to tell me that the monk he was taking me to see had been a psychiatrist, a "famous" one, he said, who in middle age had joined the order and was now at work on a book about the relations between psychological and spiritual realities. "I imagine you find that interesting," he said, which I did. But I also felt slightly irritated by what I thought was a trace of condescension in his words . . . or was it flattery?

The monk into whose minimally furnished quarters I was ushered was older than I expected, in his mid-sixties I guessed, and with his large bald head and wire-rimmed glasses I could easily imagine him as having been a psychiatrist, although what kind of one became a question as soon as the abbot left and we began talking. The conversation was mostly about the book he was writing and I found myself asking him questions about the problems I continued to have in reconciling my psychic life, particularly its sexual aspects, with the imperatives, especially certain moral ones, of the Faith.

It was obvious that I expected too much from him, for when he answered in pious generalities, occasionally in platitudes, I found myself getting annoyed. And when he told me at one point, interrupting some remark of mine by shaking his big head in a movement of wonderment, that I was so fortunate, "blessed" I'm sure he said, to be Jewish, I winced in irritation and felt like asking him just what made him so sure.

But he was kind and meant well and, if he didn't help me understand myself any better, his remark about my good fortune in being Jewish touched on an awkward truth: I half believed that there was something spiritually distinguished in being a Jew and would have liked to believe that in fact I felt, spiritually, like one. But I never had. I had never prayed as a Jew except by rote, never looked toward Yahweh for succor, never davened, or been inhabited by Jewish ghosts, most certainly not by a holy one.

I felt I'd be letting this monk-psychiatrist down, and the others too, if I told them the truth. For they were all so innocent and so kind. That evening at Vespers the abbot announced to the assembled monks, some fourteen or fifteen of them of greatly varying ages, that because the monastery was so privileged to have us there they would say a special prayer concerning us, not for our salvation, or at least not because we needed help more than they did—oh, certainly not—but simply in gratitude for our having been sent to them. As I listened to the splendid chanting I recalled a scene in Rossellini's film *Paisan* where some American army chaplains come to a mountaintop monastery in Italy during the war and the monks, terrified by the presence of a Jew among the officers, pray frantically for the Lord to forgive and protect them.

Apart from the fanfare over my Jewishness something else about those two days stays in my memory. Soon after I got there I began to have contradictory feelings, sometimes violently so, about the monks and their lives, so extraordinarily unrelated to anything in my experience. As I thought about them I would find myself respecting and even envying a little their austerity and hardiness, the nearly total erasure—or so it seemed to me—of their egos, the way life at the monastery went on with such apparent serenity. Naturally I didn't know about any inner struggles or disorder, or about any outward ones for that matter.

When I watched them during Vespers and as they filed out afterward, still chanting, the line of white-cowled figures looking like a medieval frieze or rather, it comes to me now, strangely enough like Orozco's painting *Los Zapatistas*, or when I became aware at other times of the astounding silence of the place, all sounds having moved inward, I had some transitory thoughts that perhaps this was a life I could or ought to have. For a moment I saw myself in the robe, with a tonsure, walking along with my head bowed, my hands clasped in prayer, the world remote and without significance, and God, in this harsh, beautiful, dreamlike place, very near.

But the vision was swiftly replaced by one of myself alone in a cabin, day after day, year after year, growing old (one of the monks was in his nineties) and doing what? I'd never been able to pray for more than two or three minutes at a time maybe once or twice a day, nor could I meditate for much longer. And I saw myself not being allowed to talk to anyone except once a week, but even then, talk about what? Beyond that I would be deprived of movies (that came to me first!) and music and traveling and most foods, especially meat, and liquor and even beer, and tobacco—the list grew endless and culminated in, or was overshadowed from the start by, the worst deprivation of all, sex, *any* connection to women. I felt almost faint at the prospect: exile, the desert, Siberia, death-in-life!

But after that, every shred of desire for the life of a monk having been plucked out, I had the thought that maybe I wouldn't have any say in the matter. What if it were God's will that I become a monk, as it had clearly been for Thomas Merton? I had learned the bedrock lesson that you were supposed to listen for God's word as it affected you directly; you had to be alert for signs of His intentions as they concerned you and be prepared to obey and follow them. For what kind of a deity would He be if He only made suggestions which you were free to consider or not? Of course you were always free to disobey His commands, but they *were* commands and you couldn't casually weigh them, pick among them or offer counterproposals.

And then I remembered an incident that had taken place a couple of years before my baptism at a time when I didn't have the slightest conscious interest in religion. I was in Italy and had come to Florence and gone to visit a monastery at Fiesole in the hills. My interest in going there had been purely cultural, part of my desire to see everything, for I was completely in love with Italy and wanted to go into every corner. A monk showed us around, a funny little man with birdlike mannerisms who answered my many questions (I was a sedulously inquiring traveler) with candor and a frequent odd little laugh. When toward the end of the tour I asked him how many monks were there he said, "Twenty-two . . . with you there'll be twenty-three." I remember being disconcerted and amused and protesting in mock horror. But now in retrospect the incident took on the possibility of having been a portent.

For weeks after I got back to New York I lived in terror—it's not too strong a word for what I felt—that the visit to the Carthusians, with my flicker of desire for the life there, had been the first in a series, the second if I counted the Italian incident, of communications and directives from above. But there weren't any more, or any that I could decipher, and after a while I began to breathe more easily.

And so the question of God's plans for me remained unsettled. If I wasn't to be a priest or monk, then what was I supposed to do? I didn't know if it was theologically correct to think this way, but it seemed to me that you found yourself in a set of circumstances, with one or another talent or skill, and as long as it wasn't clearly inimical to your salvation, as long as it lay within the reasonable order of human work and community, you did what you could with what you had and trusted that it would be acceptable. The word "vocation" means a calling, and while it's specifically used to denote a summoning to the formal religious life it's also of course a secular term. I'd become more than ever sure that applied to me it meant that I was "called" to be a writer.

As I've said, for months after my baptism I had suppressed the desire but it gradually stole back and before I'd been at *Jubilee* very long had become irresistible. After my debacle as a door-to-door salesman I told Ed Rice what I wanted and he began to find things for me to do. At first they were at the extreme edge of intellectual endeavor—little editing jobs, writing house ads and subscription letters for the magazine—but quite soon I was asked to do some short book and movie reviews and then given article assignments, of which the story about the Carthusian monastery was one.

After a while I became an editor. I worked ten and twelve hours a day, made sixty dollars a week as my highest salary and, at one point, along with Rice, was responsible for probably half the writing in most issues. In order to handle this we used half a dozen pseudonyms between us; one of mine that I remember was Haldon Whey, which struck me as a fine-sounding Great Plains name on the order of Hamlin Garland, and one of his was Boris Yampolsky, an authority on Russian and Greek Orthodox matters.

I wrote articles on the Spanish explorers and settlers in the American Southwest, on Joan of Arc and Thomas More, my patron saints, and on Charles de Foucauld, the saintly hermit of the North African desert. For a while I wrote a column which, at Bob Lax's suggestion, I called "Poor Richard's Gilmanack." And I reviewed all sorts of books, among them a volume of remarkable short stories by a nearly unknown southern writer named Flannery O'Connor; like almost everyone else I thought at first that she was a man. (A shy thank-you note from her for my words of praise came to the office enclosed with a subscription renewal and led to a friendship that lasted until her death.)

And so for a while, my immediate hunger to write having been appeased, I was pretty much content with and even excited by what I was doing at the magazine, sustained, as we all were, by the belief that our work was important. We were bringing new ideas to the life of the Church, raising its consciousness, as we would now say; we were arguing and demonstrating that Catholicism didn't have to be gray, tight-lipped and xenophobic. Beyond doubt it was a quixotic enterprise, considering that the magazine's circulation never went above thirty or thirty-five thousand and that we were preaching mostly to the already converted. But our exuberance held up, and to this day I occasionally meet someone who remembers the magazine with pleasure and testifies to the influence it had.

I was an associate editor of *Jubilee* for several years, from 1955 to 1959, and not the least of the benefits I got from the job was the sharpening, the creation really, of my style. I had to learn to write all over again, to write most often to order, for an occasion, on a *subject*, and this had the virtue of curbing my literariness, my romantic belief that the only true point in writing was to express the self in whatever way one could. But those articles and reviews and essays *were* myself—whose else could they have been?—and even though I still wanted a more refulgent name, a wider platform, I knew I had to serve an apprenticeship. It was a humbling experience in many ways, which of course fitted in with my general mood of abnegation. For I had recovered that morale on the whole, so that these years at *Jubilee* were perhaps the time I was best able to keep in balance the warring claims of piety and ambition. It was also the time when I was most conscientious, if not most ardent, as a Catholic.

Chapter 4

T HE "HIGH" OF A RELIGIOUS EXPERIENCE LIKE MINE
greatly resembles a love affair at its outset, as the respective comings-down resemble each other. I think of
such familiar phrases as these: to be smitten, to be swept off
one's feet, to be head over heels in love. The vision is of
gloriously wounded figures tumbling over and over, bounc-
ing to great heights, straining like balloons against their teth-
ers.

Well, you recover or decline from that bounciness, set-
tling down for the long haul, and that word, haul, reflects a
wisdom we all share: life is much heavier, less airborne than
passion makes it seem. After my first infatuation with the
Faith, which was never blind, though ardent enough, I had
to come down. I dislike the contemporary expression "to
work" at a marriage or other relationship—it suggests Con
Edison men around a street excavation—but there's a bit of
truth in it. I had to start working at being a Catholic once the
period of romance, the honeymoon, was over.

After going to Mass every day in Colorado Springs, in
New York I began to go less often, though still three or four
times a week and of course on Sundays. For a while I
shopped around for a church I could feel as comfortable in as
I had at the Mexican one in the Springs, but those that I

could find, usually small, austere and with pastors I knew and respected, were far from my apartment or the office (once in a while I'd make my way to St. Thomas the Apostle up near Columbia; I can't remember the pastor's name but he was someone committed to "social justice") so I mostly settled for the big, nondescript, businesslike places that were within reach, such as St. Ignatius or St. Jean Baptiste on Lexington and Seventy-sixth.

As long as I didn't have any sins on my conscience that I considered or knew to be mortal I went to Confession at irregular intervals, maybe every two or three weeks, and I continued to take Communion at nearly every Mass I attended. I prayed frequently enough, if most often in small motions, like exhalations or asides, and observed Fridays and Lent scrupulously, making the notable sacrifice, as I thought it to be in my case, of giving up meat. In all, I imagine that anyone studying me during this year or two, some graduate student in the sociology of religion perhaps, would have seen an unexceptional Catholic, neither perfunctory nor aflame.

During this time I finally began to look with some rigor at what I believed, as distinct from what I was supposed to believe, to explore what being a Catholic meant to me, *in itself*, apart from the differences it had made between my past and present lives in society and the changes it had brought to the way I thought of myself in the world. I had been drawn to the act of being baptized not so much by the Church's moral system or its theory of behavior (as one might call it) as by its teaching about mortality and immortality, the promise it held out of eternal life, and also by its vision and explanation of existence at its root, what it taught about the differences between Being and being, Creator and created.

Now I needed to examine how I truly felt about a number of propositions and, in a most crucial sense, *persons:* Christ—did I love Him in the way a Christian should, or at all?—Mary and the saints, God as the Father and not abstractly as the deity or first source. When I ritually said the words "Domine, non sum dignis" did I really believe I was unworthy? If so, of what and why? Did I believe in the Devil? In Purgatory, Hell? The entire moral life, sin, especially sexual sins but all the rest of them, mortal and otherwise: how had being a Catholic changed me in thought and behavior, beyond having given me a new vocabulary and a much more acute sense of the consequences of all my actions?

I wrote before that the very name "Christ" (and to an only slightly lesser degree "Jesus") had much disturbed me in my childhood and early youth. At first it had been a name without a physiognomy or a history attached to it; it had reached my awareness as a bad sound, a patch of darkness or, at best, an unpleasant expletive on the order of "God dammit!" or "Go to hell!" As I grew older it became more specific and referential: a cheap, mass-produced crucifix I saw somewhere, the limp body seeming for all the presumable agony to hang there primly; a sentimental painting in some book, Jesus blessing the multitude, His blandness and effeminacy doing nothing to dispel the vague sense of menace He gave off.

Later, in high school and college, I had learned about Christ in a formal way (in a history course and one in "comparative religion") and though He had remained a rather repellent figure, "unsavory" is the best way I can put it, the fear He'd once evoked in me dropped away. Something I bring to mind now is that from the time I began to look at Him without psychic distress I never regarded Christ as a mythical figure; though I had difficulty understanding why some Jews of His era had accepted Him as the Messiah, I never questioned His historical reality. He was either God, as He claimed, or a liar or a madman—which is what I think I believed—but He wasn't an invention.

When I read the Gilson book I must have been ready to believe in God, but that wasn't the same thing as believing in Christ as more than a man who had lived and died in a bizarre drama two thousand years ago. Yet as I write these words I'm at once aware that for Catholics, for all Christians, Christ *is* God, and really I've known this all along. But there are levels and intensities and kinds of belief, and while at the time of my baptism I had no trouble at all in accepting God's existence I had difficulty at first in giving more than the most minimal assent to Christ's existence as God. I had to try to balance in my mind and absorb the implications of those sets of paradoxical truths: that Jesus was at the same time both man and God, that God was Jesus and the Father, and that both were the Holy Spirit.

It took me awhile. For one thing I had at first to overcome my natural suspicion, as a Jew, of Christ as the enemy, the emblem of enmity and persecution. But in the other direction while I could readily imagine Christ in bodily form—after repainting the portrait so as to get rid of the languor and effeminacy—the way I usually thought of God the Father was as Michelangelo's figure on the Sistine Chapel ceiling, and what I most often saw in my mind when I summoned up that image was chiefly the finger miraculously touching Adam into life.

If I sometimes found myself praying to that finger, the way I imagine some people pray to a long white beard, in time I did address God as the Father, holding with Him a one-sided conversation made up of petitions, promises, assertions of remorse, queries and occasional rebukes for His neglect of me. As for Christ, it took longer but I became able to pray to Him too; it was often a little easier, in fact, since there was a person there, a being with a history, with flesh, hair, eyes. (Which is one of the main reasons, I'm sure, why God the Father decided to become incarnate in Christ: to make it easier, make it possible really, for us to have a connection with His own self, a self not altogether unlike our own, instead of leaving us with only a principle or a voice on the wind.)

Yet it wasn't and isn't just a question of belief. There's the matter of love, of love and belief in mutuality and reciprocity, which is one big difference between religion on the one hand and either superstition or philosophy on the other. I'm not sure whether I loved God or not, or rather I could never gauge the quality and depth of the love I certainly did feel at times. I felt it. I remember moments when the entire series of miraculous gifts, the Creation, the Incarnation and Redemption, those agencies of forgiveness and renewal, would rest with powerful lucidity in my mind, so that I would feel an overwhelming gratitude toward the events and their author. And isn't gratitude a large component of love? We can say that love is gratefulness for another's existence, can't we?

Still, I knew there was something specious in this argument. Yes, I felt grateful to God, and yes, gratefulness testifies to love, but as I moved from such generalities to the explicit injunctions and expectations of the Faith a major difficulty set in. There had to be a relationship: to this *person*, this other, to a body, the body on the Cross. The Church stressed that Christ had sacrificed supremely for us by taking on our sins and dying for them, and how could I not know that this was basic to the uniqueness of Christianity and underlay the majesty and generosity of its claim and offering? My gratitude entered in here, but once again, as so often during my time of belief, abstractly at first, as a theorem. When I thought about the Crucifixion something in me balked at feeling what I was supposed to feel, something I would later see as a mean temptation to withhold my love but at first regarded as a compelling reason for refusing it.

I knew that at the time crucifixion was the usual way of putting common criminals to death. And I couldn't at first see why Christ's suffering and ignominy were any greater than those of other crucified men, the two thieves who flanked Him, for example. More than that I kept comparing His suffering to the monstrous pain of the tortured slain Jews and other victims of the Nazis. Hadn't that been worse? For at least Jesus knew He was God and would be taken from the tomb on the third day to be brought back into Heaven, restored to His kingdom and made eternal again.

Whereas the Jews, suffering fearfully in the body, must at the same time have undergone the most appalling spiritual desolation. Whether each and every one of the victims underwent this is beside the point; surely most of them did and for all, for us too in retrospect, the horror was there to be gone through; it had been added to the world and would forever remain as history and nightmare. They had been abandoned, God had vanished, all light, hope and humanness itself had been annihilated. At least, I thought, Christ knew of the Plan, the purpose of His suffering. What plan lay behind the agony of the Nazis' victims, what purpose?

Thinking about this led me in time to the gravest, darkest, most intractable and persistent question of all: how can there be a God in a world where such evil is visited upon the innocent? (It's a supreme understatement to say that I didn't think I was engaging in an original inquiry.) In time I would find my own precarious answers: free will, our guilt and not His, Hitler as an emanation from all of us. I labored and twisted and split hairs, arguing with myself; but I finally had to ride past the ghastly dilemma on the back of faith. But before that and independent of it I had come to see how wrong, how meanly logical or analytic I had been about Christ's redemptive suffering.

I said that Jesus knew He was God, which knowledge surely would have sustained Him during the ordeal. But He couldn't have known or why would He have asked, "My God, my God, why hast thou forsaken me?" Yet He also promised the good thief that "this night thou shall be with me in paradise," so He did know. In this contradiction I came to see the truth I held on to from then on: as God He knew and as man He didn't. It followed from this that His torment was real and that it was made worse on His divine side by the knowledge of human cruelty and a widespread refusal of salvation, and on His human side by the anguish of being abandoned.

I didn't try to explain this to myself or eliminate the mystery in it. For anyone to be religious—this is as good a time as any for me to say it—means to be able to accept certain things we can't know. If religion isn't mysterious in good part, if it doesn't go past reason and the reasonable, though not to deny them, no, to expand them or make up what they lose, then it's ethical culture, toward which I couldn't possibly have been tempted.

So I juggled it all and stayed with the mystery of Christ as God until He became _acceptable_ to me; a pallid, patronizing attitude, I know, but that was how it was. Or a little more. At some point I suddenly saw what I should have seen long before, which was that Christ's agony was voluntary, that He was indeed a martyr and the prototype of martyrdom. With this understanding my movement from fear and hostility through skepticism to a rudimentary and crimped sort of love was completed. Even so, I wasn't always comfortable with the intimacy this entailed and found myself praying more often to the Virgin Mary and my patron saints, especially Joan, than to either the Father or the Son directly. (I could never bring myself to pray to the Holy Spirit; I could in fact only imagine it—Him?—as a sort of aura or gas surrounding the heavenly throne.) But I knew that to pray to the saints as much as I did was acceptable, for that was one thing they were for.

From the time I had found myself knowing the Hail Mary by heart without having learned it I would say the prayer quite often, on occasion as the penance imposed by most confessors but more often of my own volition, as a petition or a guardian utterance, before I set off to drive on the Los Angeles freeways, for a fanciful example, or when my plane seemed to be in trouble or someone close to me was ill.

Like so many other formal prayers, though, it became a rote action, and while there's nothing wrong with that in itself—it has the virtue of a comforting regularity and continuity—the fixed words of the Hail Mary acted to restrict and cramp what I had to say to her. So I began to address her on my own, so to speak, dropping the list of her attributes, of which the prayer is largely composed, or assuming them and devising my own language. In the case of Joan, for whom there's no set form of address, I was free to improvise from the start. Two women as my intercessors; I had good reason for choosing them.

The Devil. Before I became a Catholic I had had the usual humanist or secular disbelief in such a creature but I also remember having been struck by Baudelaire's sober witticism that "the Devil's first trick is to convince us that he doesn't exist." And shortly after my baptism I read and was impressed by Denis de Rougemont's book *The Devil's Share*. As I recall it, de Rougemont, a Swiss Protestant who also wrote an elegantly intelligent treatise on passion and marriage called *Love in the Western World*, argued, on Baudelaire's lines, that not to believe in Satan diminished both the drama of moral life and the substance of theology in its attempt to account for evil. Yet I was never quite persuaded and so, as I think must be true of a good many people, such credence as I gave to Satan rested less on a conviction that he truly existed than on a fear of being vulnerable to him in case he did. It was rather like Pascal's wager applied in reverse to God's enemy.

Whenever I did think of Mephistopheles (he has more names than God!) I never saw him in his conventional appearance—the forked tail, the cloven hoof and the pitchfork—but, if anything, as the modern figure of the suave business-suited man of the world, which is something of a convention by now too, I suppose. But even though I didn't rule him out I also didn't find myself assigning all that much blame to him.

To think of the Devil, the way some fundamentalists do, as having his powerful hand in a great range of evils, from pornography to the menace of "Godless" Russia, seems to me and seemed when I was a practicing Catholic to be using him as a scapegoat or, more damaging to our dignity and moral integrity, as an alibi. This doesn't mean that I thought he wasn't involved in evil—what would be his point in that case?—but that I saw him not as a maleficently creative being but as something like a principle or faculty or, more palpably, as the functionary who stamps "approved" on the wickedness we ourselves do.

To talk of the Devil is to talk of Hell and there I didn't have any problems. I believed from the beginning in Hell, though once again it wasn't in any of the traditional versions, not even that of Dante, whose taxonomy of damnation had affected me long before I suspected that Heaven and Hell might exist as more than metaphors. No, it wasn't a matter of fire and ice, physical torment of any sort, but of absence, eternal loss. I knew that this was the doctrinal teaching of the Church (did it tolerate the cruder physical versions because they were more intimidating reminders?): Hell is the everlasting separation from God, together with an acute consciousness of the loss. I accepted this from the start.

I suppose then that it was a measure of my love of God, or at least of my dread of losing Him, that during this period the most terrifying condition I could imagine being in was to have eternal life, the gift I had so recklessly craved, but have it with the unending anguish of knowing that I was forever excluded from the happiness it was supposed to give us. (I remember once comparing the desolation this would surely bring with what I had felt one time as a teenager when I hadn't been asked to a party to which everyone I cared about in my circle of friends had been invited; a frivolous, indeed probably blasphemous, analogy on the face of it, but the emotional life isn't good at making objective judgments, and whatever its cause, despair feels like you've been drained of all your blood each time it comes.) If God existed and you were cut off from Him, what else would that be but Hell? Sartre said in *No Exit* that Hell is others, but wouldn't they have to be others who have also cut themselves off from God and are therefore your appalling allies?

Which brings me at last to sin. I haven't spoken about it very much so far: a few pages on the understanding of it I got from some Catholic novelists, remarks here and there about the state of my soul in regard to Communion and Confession. During the months following my entrance into the Church I had been remarkably free of mortal sin, as far as I could determine (and I was a tough judge, never giving myself the benefit of any doubt), and at bottom I hadn't thought of my conversion as primarily the redemption of a "sinner."

But of course I had been one and would be one again, so that as the newness of being a Catholic wore off, as the period of my high flying, during which time I was convinced that I'd been sustained by updrafts of Grace, came to an end, the idea and actuality of sinfulness began to return to me, slowly and sporadically at first and then with growing rapidity and insistence. It was sin that cut you off from God both now and in futurity, and though I don't think I was deficient in an awareness of the injury sin caused to other people—that was indeed the chief way you injured God—I nevertheless thought more directly about the effect my sins would have on my relationship with Him than I did about my potential victims.

The truth is you can't separate the two things, except that sins against the Holy Spirit, despair, for example, may be said to skip over the intricate moral connections we have with one another and go straight to the source, in a denial of goodness itself. Still, as I say, when I began to sin again (how odd and comical that sounds; as though I were resuming a bad habit!) I was distressed most by the danger it posed to my chances of salvation, which I suppose is as it should be for believers. Yet it leaves a vulnerable place for the charge unbelievers make: that a moral system legislated, policed and rewarded by an otherworldly being can work to diminish your sense of responsibility in this world and undermine or corrupt the desire to do good for its own sake or that of others.

I reach for my dictionary and find this definition: "Deadly sins, _in theology_, the seven capital sins (pride, covetousness, lust, anger, gluttony, envy and sloth); so called because regarded as causing spiritual death." For me the seven readily fall into several categories, or rather one of them, lust, immediately separates itself out. I can't defend it to the satisfaction of either psychologists or logicians, to say nothing of theologians, but I thought then and still do that lust was of a different order from the others, that it was the most problematic sin if by no means the worst. At any rate it was the one that sent me most frequently and agitatedly into battle with my conscience and the commandments of the Faith, the one in whose territory I found it hardest to reconcile nature and the supernatural.

Surely I was, and am, far from being alone in this. We all know that much of the seepage from membership in the Church, including the dropping away of priests and nuns, has for a long time been due to sexual dilemmas and despair. There are more than enough traps or swamps to fall into: adultery, premarital sex, abortion, masturbation, homosexuality, birth control, "perversions." Those subcategories (have I left any out?) all fall under the rubric of "lust," and apart from the use of contraceptives and the practice of abortion, which most often have highly rational bases, are distinguished from the other deadly sins and their particularities by the fact that the impulse which leads to them, the energy which keeps them in motion, is so largely unconscious.

I summon to memory the mortal sins, apart from lust, as they lounged about waiting for me to commit them, and the act of recollection fills out and supports my argument. To begin with I was never slothful during this time, quite the contrary, so this particular sin doesn't figure. As for the others, I found it possible to combat them, if not thoroughly rout them, each time they beckoned, since I could engage in a lively skirmishing with temptation by drawing on my will and reason the way I did in other areas. And in this warfare Catholicism was for a while a dependable ally and supplier of arms.

When I found myself being envious or covetous I told myself that it was spiritual blessings I ought to crave and not worldly objects or status; when my normal appetite threatened to turn into gluttony I called up models of austerity from the lives of holy people; when I was proud I brought to mind that the last shall be first and when I was angry I reminded myself that the meek will inherit the earth.

This all sounds mechanical and pat, I know, and in truth my struggle for a moral life that would go beyond the utilitarian and self-serving was most often tempestuous and disorderly. And it was never easy. Pride, the most subtle of sins, was especially troublesome, having continually to be admonished and pushed down, but not too far, not so far that it would turn into that strident kind of self-abasement which is vanity in the guise of its opposite.

But the point was that I could use my reason and goodwill against all the mortal sins, could hold more or less effective dialogues with temptation, so to speak. Except, after a while, for lust. (Hamlet: "Except my life. Except my life." He means that he has hold of everything save what matters.) And this is like saying that in the crucial arena, where sin was most likely to occur for me, I was nearly unarmed.

I've always thought the word "lust" greatly inadequate and seriously misleading as a descriptive for the cluster of acts and thoughts and fantasies that make up the formal sin. It connotes hard breathing and pounding veins, cupidity, leering, an itch. But at least as often there's melancholy and the sense of being ensnared, a victim; at least as often, too, love is present in the sin, as it never is in envy or gluttony, say. And the sense of sad, ecstatic mortality.

But for all this the Church knew what it meant by lust and I knew it too. What we both chiefly knew, if for different reasons we didn't dare to explicate, was that the whole realm of sexuality is a threat to spirituality and transcendence; its pleasures are so intensely of this world, so intolerant of postponement, that in their sway the long view shrinks and disappears, the sense of eternity collapses into

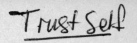

the body *at this moment*, the flesh urging its prerogatives. In regard to birth control I've come to think that the Church's most profound objection to it isn't so much that it prevents life as that it testifies to the primacy of pleasure and the consequent refusal of creaturely responsibility.

So there's the topography of my moral life during the two or three years after my baptism: stretches of untroubled ground spotted with occasional patches of quicksand and here and there a gully if not a chasm. My fight was most often with lust and then with pride and then, probably, envy, and so on down through the list. But all in all for many months I felt in control, felt that I could trust myself and rely on what was *trusting me*. And then things began to change.

It's a Saturday afternoon in late summer or early fall, two or three years after my baptism. I'm sitting in a coffee shop a block or two from the church, St. Vincent Ferrer on Lexington and Sixty-fifth, where I've just gone to Confession. Mechanically stirring the sugar in my cup I go over what happened a few minutes ago in the Box and feel a sudden tremor of apprehension, a flicker of premonition that makes me shake my head to try to drive it away. Because of what's just taken place, for the first time since my baptism I can imagine not being a Catholic, not being able to remain one.

My wife and I had lived apart for a year after my return to New York, had then resumed our marriage and were living now in an atmosphere that was slowly increasing in tension and discord. A few months before we'd come back together she too had been baptized. I don't know if it was a profound conversion, one based on conviction and deep longing, or, at least in part, an effort in my direction and toward saving the marriage. Whatever it was, I honored what she did then and honor it now, but I don't think that becoming a Catholic was

195

ever as radical or deep-seated a change for her as it was
for me.

Oddly enough, though I welcomed and encouraged it, her
joining me in this way put added pressure on me since it implied that she'd trusted what I had done and now looked to
me for guidance and exemplary acts. This took many forms,
but since the sexual area, the dominion of Lust in Catholic
terms, had been where most of our marital plagues seemed
to breed, it was there that I was expected to have changed
most thoroughly. And I *had* changed, if my celibacy and
strict supervision and control of my erotic fantasies during
the year following my baptism were a valid measure.

Later I would begin to think it hadn't been. For during
that year something I have at least in hindsight to call "artificial" reigned: under the sway of divinity and with its almost palpable assistance the ratio in me of mind or spirit to
body shifted heavily toward the former so that I was either
untroubled by carnal yearnings or, when on occasion they'd
make themselves felt, I could suppress the "illegitimate" in
them. The incident with the prostitute in New Orleans had
been followed by many months of asceticism—I was about
to say "self-denial," but there was really nothing much to
deny.

And so for a while things went fairly well. We were both
sustained at first by the energy that came from her conversion, a primary infusion for her and a replenishment for me.
I brought her into the Catholic community I now inhabited,
where she made some friends and moved without apparent
strain, if not with the fullest enthusiasm, her Jewish-atheist
background being perhaps a little more resistant to the cultural change than mine had been.

Surprisingly, though, there was a brief period when
she seemed more ardent in her faith than I was in mine, or
anyway more zealous in observing it. Or maybe it wasn't

so surprising. She had been instructed and baptized by a priest famous in the neighborhood for his piety and eloquence, a Father Thibodeau, who put me in mind of certain seventeenth-century French preachers, notable fishers of souls, stern, learned confessors. His influence on her didn't last very long but while it was there she outdid me in some devotional ways.

One evening I went with her to St. Jean Baptiste for a lecture by Father Thibodeau, one of a series he was giving on some such topic as "How to Be a Catholic in a Secular World." We got there a few minutes early and I looked around the rapidly filling room. In a chair at the back I suddenly saw *her*, Ruth. With my heart flapping in my chest I swiveled through the aisles, reached her and, the words tumbling out, said something like this: "Ruth, it's me, I'm a Catholic, I was baptized two years ago, I made you my godmother secretly (which I had), I'm sorry for running away, it's so wonderful to see you, I . . . ."

Before I could finish I became aware that she was looking at me coldly, as though at a stranger or, worse, someone out of a distressing past. She said nothing and I backed away, after mumbling something like "What's the matter, I don't understand." I still don't. For a while I tried to and then, so painful and unsettling were all the possible explanations, I gave it up. So Ruth, dear dear Ruth, who were you and what was I to you? I'll never forget you, but what am I to remember?

For some months my wife and I managed to get along, the only major source of friction being the growing dissatisfaction we both felt about our lack of real careers. And then the first signs began to appear of a partial reversion to the past. I found myself being visited by emissaries from that side of my sexual nature which had figured in our earlier dissonance. Wraithlike at first, offering pale solicitations, they became more substantial after a while.

As I write these words a mad image of Jekyll and Hyde shapes itself in my mind. I see myself, a clear-faced, youthfully decent-looking man in my early thirties, beginning to turn into a beast, hair growing down my forehead and over my cheeks, my nose broadening and flattening, my lips swelling, the points of fangs starting to push through my gums. I drive the dopey clichéd image away but it comes back and, I tell myself, at least has had the virtue of indicating how internally divided I had once again begun to feel.

I find that more and more in these pages I've been making a division between the "natural" and the supernatural. Sometimes I've meant simply the difference between the secular and the religious, but more pointedly the separation is between myself without God and with Him. As long as I was attached to the divine and it, He, kept a hand and eye on me I was more than my natural self, protected from its treacheries, but if that hand and gaze were lifted from me I'd fall back into nothing more than "nature." And I began to fear that this might be happening.

During my first year or so as a Catholic I had been able to be both celibate and "normal" in my carnal desires and I thought this was due to the working of Grace. I haven't used the word "Grace" very often in these pages and find that strange, since its meaning is so pertinent to my case. Grace is the principle or action above and beyond physical nature, including your own of course. It's the action by which divinity lifts the believer toward itself, dispels his or her melancholy, gives strength to endure and persevere; indeed Grace is what makes it possible to believe in the first place.

I'd been taught that and experienced it too. And I'd also been taught that Grace would always be given to you if you prayed for it with sincerity. But when the beast in me began to assert itself again it seemed that my power to ask for help, for Grace, grew weaker and weaker, or the more likely truth is that I couldn't pray *sincerely*.

I think of the line from Augustine that figured in the dream with which this book began: "God, send me chastity . . . but not yet." That's being insincere, that's asking for the blessing *later*, after you've sneaked in just a few more submissions to temptation. I suppose it was true, though I couldn't see it, that I moved on such a devious course, half honest and half not, my mind or eye or heart or conscience or some faculty or other fixed on reformation and renewed "purity" but my body reaching for its immediate and outlaw satisfactions.

The *beast* in me? Was I really so bad? I had fantasies, dreamed of muscular women (poor child, I was born a generation too soon; they're all around now, licit and glowing!), I secretly read pornography from time to time and every so often masturbated (*"Eh bien, lis, dévore, et branle-toi"*— "Well, then, read, devour, and masturbate," Mirabeau exhorted the reader of his privately printed erotic book, *Ma Conversion*).

Once in a while I went to prostitutes, most of whom I found in a wide-open bar called La Fiesta on West Forty-sixth Street or here and there in Greenwich Village. In regard to my wife I lacked masculine assertiveness (as of course, technically, fidelity; though I didn't have any affairs, which I thought made some difference), couldn't get into the missionary position very often, was impotent now and then, and wanted games and exotic paraphernalia (stockings, garter belts and high heels: the old *Blue Angel* mise-en-scène) but was too ashamed to ask her to wear them.

There was nothing extreme in my desires, or at any rate such extremities as I went to in my fantasies (to be the slave of an Amazon queen, say) remained there, in a realm of ideal possibility, such as philosphers attend to with logic and such as the rest of us, not so analytical or disinterested, dreamily invoke a dozen times a day in many mental regions besides the erotic.

I didn't want to hurt or be hurt. I think I can say that I was essentially a gentle person; in regard to women I was certainly the opposite of macho. But I inflicted hurt anyway, in this area at least, by, as I saw it, withholding myself in crucial ways, dispersed among the landscapes of sexual reverie, unable to take my place within the rhythms of ordinary desire or to obey the imperatives of constancy and fidelity, openness and mutual trust.

And yet . . . was the real source of our marital discord sexual and, for that matter, was sex, its "warping," its having strayed from the accepted track, wholly behind my own psychic disorder and distress? Trouble *shows itself* in sex, always: energy may be lost there, where it ought to be regained, emotions that should expand may be crimped or made chaotic, selfishness can thrive and obsessions, which in their pursuit temporarily obliterate all other reality, can send "values" flying. Still, couldn't there have been something in my being, some different if related "trouble," for which sexual desires and acts were evidence but not absolute cause?

Kierkegaard wrote that most unhappiness in adult life is the result of a mental "mistake" in childhood, some great and fatal misreading of nature and the world. Through psychoanalysis and other means I was to learn later something about my own mistake, and it included sex but wasn't coterminous with it. I reach for my notes and find this remark of Denis de Rougemont: "Most so-called 'sexual' neuroses have their genesis in . . . the soul's rejection of the body taken as the sign and symbol of the self's 'prison.' "

Once again the soul and the body. Manichaeanism: fatal opposition. I felt imprisoned by the body, by its specificity, its aggressions (particularly the male body's aggressions, which I inverted), the way it stayed impervious to values other than its own. I didn't see that to live between values on the one hand and reality on the other is deadly. I didn't know that the body may be surmounted, if that's what you wish, but only through love, or that my sexual life wasn't in itself evil, but that the selfishness with which I pursued it, the solipsism of its dream-substance, were.

Yet this knowledge came long after the time I'm writing about, and in those days all I could see was that sex was the chief source of my psychic and moral turmoil and of our marriage's foundering.

Even so, there were moments during those years when I thought (as there are times when I think now) that goodwill and generosity on both our parts might have carried us across the bog to some sort of firmer conjugal ground. I wrote earlier in the book that I thought my wife and I were incompatible, and so in all likelihood we were. But that was in the "natural" world and what does it mean? We weren't of different species nor were we substances that chemically, organically, simply won't mix. We had minds, souls, and these were agencies of possible triumph over such implacability; we could *will* our way to compatibility, we could pray our way to it.

So the Church had taught us and for a long while we both believed it. That it never really worked didn't keep us from trying, both in sex and in all those matters beyond it for which sex is blamed and serves as a scapegoat: in our case there were accusations of selfishness and lack of responsibility, jealousies, warring vocabularies—the clashing names we gave to our emotions and behavior—refusals to make allowances and sheer incomprehensions. We addressed ourselves to all of this, for a time doggedly and then sporadically, until the defeat was unmistakable. But before that another, larger defeat had been set in motion for me.

I can't remember anything like the exact sequence of internal events nor can I do much better with the external ones, but what I do recall is that the crisis began obliquely on a day when for the first time since my baptism I found myself balking at the idea of having to go to Confession. I'd never exactly relished stepping into the Box, but up to now as long as my sins, even rather grave ones, were spiritual and not corporeal, acts of the mind and not the body—more precisely temptations of the ego, not the id—I went to confess them without much fuss.

Though it wasn't at all clear to me at the time, I made the distinction on the basis of an idea that spiritual sins were the special province of priests, who could be expected to have more or less supple knowledge of them, whereas sins of the flesh, sexual ones anyway, lay outside their competence. A foolish distinction, perhaps, but as my sins of "lust" grew more frequent and especially when they took on the quality of actuality instead of dream—a visit to a prostitute, for example, or an act of masturbation—I found it harder and harder to confess them.

I spoke of it being a foolish separation, this drawing of a line between the body and the spirit in the realm of immorality, and abstractly or theologically I'm sure it was. For Christ had certainly said, "He who lusts after a woman in his heart has already committed adultery." Yet from the time my period of celibacy ended I had some justification for that dividing line, the same sort of justification so many other Catholics have felt themselves to have in this area, when the dilemmas of the body, its entanglements of need, desire and moral obligation are so often met with incomprehension, rigid codes and mechanical censure.

When I began to have to confess "impure" thoughts I was more often than not asked questions like "How many times have you committed this sin?" (I remember one occasion when after I'd replied, "Four times, Father," I had to resist the temptation to amend that with, "No, three and a half, I nipped one of them in the bud"), and "Are you married?" (this of course to ascertain if I was a first- or second-degree wretch), and "Do you take brisk walks or cold showers at such times?" (twice I was asked that), and when these were followed by admonitions to "rid" myself of my mental offenses against God, my irritation, doubt and uncertainty grew, the pace quickening when a few of the thoughts began to turn into action.

The annoyance and doubt had to do with whether my confessors really understood what was at issue. I mean psychologically at issue; morally they surely knew their business, or at any rate the moral business of the Church as it had been entrusted to them. But that was where the trouble lay: in the distance and sometimes enmity between moral and psychological truth, between abstract good and bodily importunity, the "higher" and the lower, transcendence and the moment.

If I could sum up in a phrase what most of my confessors seemed to lack it would be an "understanding of unconsciousness." They didn't recognize, or did but rejected the awareness, that the psyche isn't equivalent to the conscious mind; that thoughts and desires arise for us behind our backs so to speak; that there's an antagonism between the thoughts we can choose to have and those that choose us; and that you can't simply *rid* yourself of what the catechisms call "unwelcome" desires because—oh, intractability, thorniness, ruination of all "right" frames of mind!—such desires usually *are* welcome, except that the glad hand is offered in one sphere while in a neighboring one there are frowns, condemnations and slammed doors.

Nature vs. spirit, the body against the soul: once more the dichotomy reveals itself. And as I write this section I fret about how elementary everything I'm saying might be thought, how tired the notion of such an opposition might seem. Don't we all know about such things as the will at the mercy of the unconscious, haven't we always known? For that matter in our era of frantic health is the conflict still felt? Perhaps it's that there's less acknowledgment of it; maybe mind vs. body isn't so much a tired idea as a cranky one in an age of therapy.

Exhausted or not the idea was there for me in those days, the fact was there and held me in its grasp, as it continues to do. It's less tenacious now, being partly a memory, since I've stopped trying to heal the split between soul and body. Or rather I've changed the terms. God is no longer a factor, so for my survival—what time remains to me up to the point where eternity either sets in or it doesn't—I've taken to trying to ride with the inner animosities or ceding their mystery to the care and inquiry of psychiatry whenever, as happens often, the contrarieties of my being start really clawing at one another.

At the time I'm writing about, the mystery of will vs. impulse was fiercely present and it consumed me as I fought to hold on to my faith. Didn't the priests who heard my confessions see the problem and respect its obduracy? Couldn't they acknowledge this particular enemy's presence? "That which I would do I do not do, that which I would not do I do," Saint Paul wrote, lamenting his incapacitated will. Didn't those priests know about that? Ah, please, a lit-

tle humility: of course they did, or anyway the truth it reflected. They weren't entirely ignorant of the way the psyche worked.

There were even some priests at the time who'd had psychiatric training or at least instruction (there are more of
them now), though I never met any. And there were a few
Catholic psychiatrists and psychoanalysts, who labored
strenuously and, I now think, probably with a degree of despair, to reconcile the truths of the Faith with those of carnality. I went to see one later in this period. He was a
famous man, Dr. Gregory Zilboorg, a tall, saturnine European who made me think of Bela Lugosi with a mustache.
He listened to my story without comment, told me he
couldn't take me as a patient because he was ill and getting
old and cutting down on his practice, then ushered me out of
his office with the advice, delivered in what I thought was a
rather glum or faintly skeptical tone, to pray harder and
more often.

And that was the point. Even the more understanding of
the priests I went to or encountered in the Box, the few who
after listening to my tales of waywardness and "depravity"
didn't come down on me with "humphs" and clucks and
long clearings of the throat, even these sympathetic confessors could suggest only prayer as a recourse. And they were
right to do it, I see now, for what else was there? The
Church has never been a psychiatric institution nor had I
ever really expected it to be one.

No, what troubled me at this time and in the end came to
seem insurmountable wasn't that Catholicism couldn't offer
me a "cure" but that it didn't seem willing or able to let my
conscience operate in the space between the facts of my
erotic and other malfeasances and the better part of my nature, the part that truly did want to adhere to the Word, in-

termittent as that determination may have been. The Church preaches the supremacy of conscience but in practice surrounds it with all sorts of restrictions.

As I encountered it Catholicism had no tolerance for what I suppose I have to call "situation ethics," though the term smacks of moral fashion. I wanted it to give me flexible interpretations of, and judgments on, complex inner events, but instead it applied fixed, imperious moral criteria. And this had the effect of shattering the delicate structures of simultaneous accommodation and resistance to wayward appetite that people like me tend to build as a way of being able to *keep going*. (I think it was Freud who described neurosis in some such way: as a fearful surrender of part of the self in order to preserve the rest.)

Theologically I'm sure I had it all wrong. I was caught between what I ought to have known and didn't or couldn't; I wavered between *correctness* and actuality, or two kinds of desire. And presumptuous as it might appear, I have the idea that it's the story of many other Catholics or erstwhile ones, as well as of people struggling to be religious in any faith.

On one side the living substance and workings of the Faith, the texture and density of your animate presence within it; on the other side the rules. Dogma: the very word suggests the implacable, the unforgiving. I had gone into the Church embracing dogma, but not seeing then its coldness and severity, even though I understood that there had to be rules, that it couldn't be an amateur or free-form quest. I'd wanted to shift some of the burden of selfhood onto the Laws, but now because of my inability to live wholly by them I felt I was being thrown back into the self, a victim of its sabotage, of the way, if I can say such an odd thing, it leaves you to your own devices.

I felt left to myself, abandoned after having been *in touch*, sustained by something I could call a collaboration, an alli-

ance, and surely all those recommendations and exhortations
to pray which my confessors kept heaping on me were
meant to repair that new condition of separation. So despite
my unhappiness at not being "understood" I decided to
obey, and for a while said formal prayers more frequently
than I was accustomed to doing, as well as sending many little fragmentary ad-libbed messages to Heaven throughout
the day, on the subject of my compulsions and what I would
like Them up there to do about it.

But nothing happened. I don't mean that no usable answers were forthcoming—they never are—or that I didn't
feel changed immediately—one never does—but that it all
seemed to be in a void, empty, dry, without even an echo. I
was spinning around on my own words, a verbal dervish in
the midst of uttermost silence. As I said before, perhaps I
wasn't praying sincerely, maybe I wanted to ease the guilt
but not eradicate its cause, not yet. But how can you see that
when the deception is your own work?

And there was something else that might have been a factor, an additional odd strain of possible insincerity. My old
difficulty in praying to Christ returned, in a new form: this
time I felt strangely embarrassed by the subject and content
of my murmurings and pleas, my perversion. Did I think He
didn't already know about that side of me? Did I think I'd
shock Him? Weirdly I did think so.

Part of it was the sense I shared with everyone else of His
extreme asexuality, but more specifically I thought He'd be
embarrassed by my special tastes. Since the great bulk of
biblical warnings against lust have to do with straight, traditional adultery or intercourse outside marriage, with one or
two screeds against homosexuality thrown in, I could imagine Him shaking His head at this new, "modern" deviation
from the sexual Law. It wasn't any good my thinking, well,
at least I'm not brutal, nor do I go *chasing* women, and He

ought to be softened by that; all I could see was Christ sitting on His throne with His eyes rolling in His head and all sympathy and love for me draining away.

After a time in the face of this absurdity I began to do something which to remember now fills me with a wry, tender melancholy. I turned to the Virgin Mary and Joan of Arc and prayed to them for help with my sexual problems (and other difficulties beyond the erotic, for there *were* those too). I'm touched to think I did this and want to explain my reasoning, if there was anything so clear as that.

They were women, females, upon whose sex my offenses were inflicted, or if I didn't work palpable harm—in my masochism I was after all what I thought of as a "counter-rapist"—then I offended by neglect and inadequacy, in the sphere of marriage certainly. So I prayed to these two virgins, to Mary, about whom there was so little one could know apart from her function and status, and to Joan, about whom there was so much. In long tearful soliloquies I told them how nothing in me intended harm to women, how the best part of me loved and admired them more than I did men, and how I longed to be restored, to them, to Eve, to my wife and all femininity (that flowing, gracious word).

At these times I saw the Blessed Virgin as either the radiant queen of Heaven or the sorrowing mother at the foot of the Cross, both images conventional and even hackneyed, although at the time no less affecting to me for that. And I reminded her that she had miraculously taught me the prayer created for her, or had intervened so it could happen, which meant that she was in a way especially responsible for me now.

As for Joan, she was sometimes the glorious rider in armor of my childhood infatuation, sometimes the sturdy maid with cropped hair, dressed in loose tunic and pants. But once in a while I would see her on the pyre, with the flames beginning to mount: the heartbreaking meekness in the midst of agony, the mild eyes raised unreproachfully to Heaven. And I would remember (or maybe I only do it now) the story that after the fire had consumed her a dove was seen to rise from the ashes and fly off in the direction of Paris, and that an English soldier was said to have cried out through his tears: "We have burned a saint!"

Why have I always loved Joan so? My closest friend, the painter Sherman Drexler, once suggested that she fulfilled my ideal of strength in women, that I responded equally to her robust physique and her indomitability. He meant it kindly and there's truth in his perception, but it leaves out a great deal. To begin with I scarcely allowed myself to think of Joan in an erotic way; if anything, when on a few occasions I started to have such a reverie I drove it away out of the same sense of the illicit, very nearly the sacrilegious, that is supposed to have come over the soldiers she led and fought alongside of, whenever desire for her entered their thoughts.

Beyond that, it hasn't been simply Joan the heroine, the physical heroine, that is, whom I've adored, a veneration that has led me to read everything written about her in English and a good deal in French, to make pilgrimages to Domrémy and Rouen and, in a lighter vein, to forgive the faults of Bernard Shaw's play *Saint Joan* because of the love he too had for her.

As much as I admired Joan's prowess and valor it was her final suffering and the way she bore it that endeared her to me, or rather it was the fusion in her of so noble a character with so piteous a fate. That at such an early age she should have suffered so cruel a death for being valorous, incorruptible and, in the deepest way, innocent; that she should have swayed under fear and then straightened up again; that her virtue should have been so hard and yet so crystallinely

open and generous; that she should have been so wise and so
unlettered; that she should have been so monstrously condemned and then exonerated, from the beginning in
Heaven, I'm sure, but only later on earth; that in short she
should have captured in her brief existence so many painful
antitheses and contradictory dimensions of being and destiny—for all these reasons I've loved and cherished her.

And for one other supreme reason: that she was a woman,
with all that this meant of adversity, vulnerability and,
therefore, of the unlikelihood of such deeds as hers. A few
years ago my older daughter, eight or nine at the time, asked
me out of the blue why there were so few celebrated women,
"heroes" was the word she used. I gave her the usual reasons
from social and political history, cited male prejudice, and
then, to make her and myself feel better, listed the familiar
exceptions: Mme. Curie, Amelia Earhart, Golda Meier and
so on. Then I said, "And Joan of Arc. Ah, but Joan, she was
the greatest hero of all, male or female. Do you know I think
she was the most wonderful person who ever lived?" My
daughter smiled, taking it in, perhaps even beginning to
know what to do with it.

No dramatic changes came as a result of my prayers to
Joan and Mary, but I thought I could detect a little difference, a faint lightening of the silence, the suggestion of a distant receptivity. I prefer to think I wasn't being wishful.
Anyway my wife and I struggled on. Then one day, I can't
remember at whose instigation, we decided to go to a Catholic marriage counselor. (I don't know if that was his precise
title, but advising troubled husbands and wives was what he
did.) He was a Dominican priest named Francis Wendelkin
and we went to see him one evening at his church, St. Vincent Ferrer on Lexington.

He had pale blond hair and was rotund, heavy-browed

and jowly, so that in his black cowled robe he made me think of the British actor Peter Bull miscast as Friar Tuck. There was something both unctuous and overbearing in his manner, an odd and especially unpleasant amalgam, but his personality wouldn't have mattered all that much had he offered us anything beyond denunciations (we told him that since we didn't think our marriage was strong enough to sustain a child we'd been practicing contraception, knowing it to be wrong, and he sternly ordered us to use the rhythm method instead; I don't think we ever did, nor did I ever formally confess the "sin"), platitudes and rote advice. He spoke of marriage being a sacrament and the body being "God's vessel," emphasized my responsibility as "head of the family" and told us to pray together and go on a joint retreat.

My memory of him is sour, but it's possible I'm being somewhat unfair, since he was working by his lights and as I write these lines I remember that at the time I was less contemptuous than intimidated and disappointed. I recall too that after we left I told my wife, in reference to the injunction to pray more, "Well, what have we got to lose?" Or maybe I only thought it.

So we did pray more for a while (though I'm sure it wasn't together; there was something embarrassing about that) and things went along fairly evenly for a time. Then I began to have new lapses, needed to confess them and had the idea of going to Father Wendelkin. Presumably I wanted to test him, to see what his response would be to my sins as rather more concrete and specific misdeeds than the generalized picture of disturbances I had presented to him at our session.

I was of course tempting fate, which didn't refuse the challenge. Kneeling in the confessional I told the priest, who I'm pretty sure didn't know who I was, what was on my conscience: certain intricate fantasies followed by acts of masturbation, the descriptions couched in terms halfway between euphemism and candor. He listened without comment, asked if I was married, then gave me a short stern lecture on my errant ways, repeating the themes he had stressed during our consultation (he even used the phrase "God's vessel" again), and ended by imposing as my penance a great number of Hail Marys, which I was to accompany with prolonged meditation on the Blessed Virgin's purity and my offenses against her. Naturally I wasn't about to tell him that I *had* been praying to the Virgin; the discrepancy between his sense of the matter and mine seemed too great.

So there I now was, in the coffee shop thinking things over, or rather trying to fight off my sense of hopelessness: I would never be understood, I would never be able to bring my definitions of lust and guilt, or my reading of the psyche in relation to the soul, into line with *theirs*. For whatever reason the understanding I'd once had of the instrumental nature of Confession, that its efficacy didn't depend on what the confessor was like, had disappeared; the personality, or at least the mind of the confessor, mattered to me now and, worse, I saw priests like Father Wendelkin as more and more representative of the Church itself.

Something else became true at this time. I had struggled to constrain my ambitiousness, and had mostly managed to do it, but after several years I had begun to feel renewed stirrings of worldly desires. I had passed thirty, long since disqualified as an *enfant terrible* and aware that I was well behind even the normal expectations for a writer of my age, so that I had to catch up.

As time went on I began to see the world I was exercising my talents on at *Jubilee* as much too small, and started to

Lack of Intellectualism

crave a wider one. I didn't want to be only a Catholic writer or intellectual; that was to be crimped, coerced in a certain way. Because for all the freedom we had, or thought we did, within the Church's life of perceptions and ideas, we were still on a leash, we still had to keep in mind the limits of what we could say. Doubtless I had this wrong. Later, when it was too late, I would come to see that there were supple minds who could get round, or overwhelm with brilliant verbal strategies, the Church's seeming restrictions on inquiry and expression.

I wasn't one of them. I was disturbed by a sense of things pressing from behind or below, utterances I might have made or thoughts I might have taken further, if I hadn't already given my assent to the boundaries I saw the Church as having set up. In time it became for me a question of warring realms. At the intersection in me of sex and ambition, or lust and pride, illicit desire in both cases, since foolish as it may have been I saw my craving to be well-known as illicit—at this convergence I started to chafe and grumble.

Not long ago I read a book by the late Ernest Becker called *The Denial of Death*. "Nature's values are bodily values," Becker wrote, "human values are mental values." His implication was that religious values are spiritual ones, neither bodily nor mental, and he quoted the psychoanalytic pioneer Otto Rank on the confusion a failure to recognize this distinction can bring about: "It seems so difficult for the individual to realize that there exists a division between one's spiritual and purely human needs, and that the satisfaction or fulfilment for each has to be found in different spheres." I was becoming exemplary of the inability or refusal to see this.

Chapter 5

PARIS, A COLD DRIZZLY AFTERNOON IN THE FALL OF 1957, about a year after that crisis in the coffee shop. My wife and I have been in Europe for three or four months, mostly in Spain and Italy, then through Switzerland, Germany and Holland before coming back to France. We've been living on some savings and the hospitality of friends and I've been making notes and storing up impressions for a couple of articles I intend to write for *Jubilee*, from which I've taken a leave of absence. This has been my first trip to Europe since I was baptized, so I've been especially receptive to the Catholic presence and reminders everywhere, although I've had decidedly mixed feelings.

One thing I've felt is nostalgia and, I think, how can you be nostalgic for something that hasn't happened yet? I'm still a Catholic, still practicing, if with much effort, yet in certain churches or other Catholic places, particularly in Spain, I've felt as if I were looking back at some land I once inhabited.

I think of the cathedral at Saragossa, enormous, set in a vast square that was mysteriously empty on the afternoon we were there, reminding me of a Chirico painting. It's the shrine of a "miraculous" little black statue of the Virgin, and on a pillar inside the main entrance there's a plaque, commemorating some liturgical conference, which reads: "In this immortal city of Saragossa in the year 19—" *Immortal* city! Later I saw the same stupendously self-assured words in Ávila, Saint Teresa's city, and remembered the hunger that had led me to the priest's hand and the warm water of baptism.

In response to that memory I made a pilgrimage to Unamuno's home off the main plaza in Salamanca and then, staying within the circle of eternity, went to the Escorial outside Madrid. Ah, I was moved by its atmosphere of madness and gloom, yet also lofty exaltation; it's a colossal reminder of what the Faith must once have been like and is probably still like in secret Spanish souls here and there. Death and pride . . . pride and then marble effigies.

I'm walking along the Seine just now, on the Left Bank, where our little hotel, the Saints-Pères, is (we hadn't picked it for its name). The bookstalls are closed and the river is dark green in the rain. I'm looking for a church—I thought of Notre Dame but quickly dropped the idea—where I can go to Confession, which I still do, though at longer and longer intervals. It's occurred to me that it might be easier to spill out my sins in French, as well as to absorb being chastised for them in that tongue, so I've rehearsed a number of pieces of language for the ritual: *bénissez-moi, mon père, parce que j'ai peché; je suis plein d'orgueil* (pride); *fantasies érotiques; branler* (which means "to masturbate").

What is troubling me more than anything else is whether or not I can stay a Catholic, and though this is related to my inability to reconcile my sexual nature and the Law it isn't at all confined to that, as my repertoire of sins isn't. "Confined" is an appropriate word to pop up right now, for I feel pent up in Catholicism, caged by its network of rules and commands. Already I've begun to pick among them, deciding which ones to obey and which to ignore (using birth

215

control is an example of that), and I know that if this goes further something's going to give way, some master strut, the spine of the thing. It hasn't happened yet, but there's another matter, worse in some respects. I can barely pray, or rather when I do the silence is total. I feel more and more remote from Heaven, eternal life, Christ, the Father and even Mary and Saint Joan.

I turn into a side street, walking away from the river, and suddenly come upon a nondescript little church or chapel almost hidden among the storefronts. Inside it's nondescript, too, which means it isn't especially ornate or tacky. A few people are there, shuffling about in the semidarkness or kneeling in prayer, and when I walk over to the confessional I see an elderly woman waiting near it and fingering her rosary beads; when another woman comes out she goes in. She's back in less than a minute (no moral crisis there, I think) and I take her place.

I kneel down, call on my will and recite my first phrase in French: "*bénissez-moi, mon père, parce que j'ai,*" and so on. Before I can go any further the priest on the other side of the partition says: "If it would make you feel more comfortable why not speak English? I understand and speak it very well."

I'm thoroughly disconcerted and feel a little foolish but I throw away the carefully prepared French phrases and tell him in English when my last Confession was (five or six weeks ago to an American priest at some church in Turin). Then I go through my sins, some of which are sexual, with anger and pride in there too. When I've finished listing them I decide to add in French—partly because the phrase is so elegant, though I'm not sure I've got it grammatically right—that I suffer from "*l'inquiétude dans la foix.*" The priest hasn't said anything during my recitation, but now he repeats, in English, "restlessness."

Something about the way he's handed the word back to me, as though accompanying it with a nod of recognition, immediately gives me confidence, so that before I know it I'm pouring everything out. I tell him the whole story as swiftly as I can, the salient aspects anyway, and end by describing my present state of disconsolateness, emptiness and doubt. "Aridity," I hear him say and when I ask what he means he repeats, in his slightly formal English, "aridity—that is the Church's term for your condition. You should know that I have experienced it myself."

We went on talking. I remember wondering as the minutes stretched on if I might be keeping someone else from the confessional, maybe some criminal with a real load on his conscience. But the priest didn't seem to be concerned so I wasn't either.

We spoke about literature a little (he had admired some of the same writers I had, Dostoevsky and Baudelaire, Mauriac and Bernanos) but for the most part I asked him questions concerning my dilemmas. His replies, "responses" is better, were always reflective and patient, sometimes a trifle weary, I thought, but with nothing behind them of pedagogical or priestly *authority*. Instead of preaching to me it was more as if he was sharing some speculations, some experience too, offering me his hard-won and not at all impregnable thought.

"What I've got to find out, Father," I said to him after a few minutes, "is how to believe again. I mean believe the way I once did." "And how was that?" he asked. "Fully," I said, "or almost fully. With confidence and (I cast about for the word) . . . ardor." "And now?" he asked. "Aridly," I replied, allowing myself a little smile he couldn't of course see.

"You know," he said then, "it is such a mystery how belief of the kind you describe comes and goes. We cannot know why we have it—except that it comes through Grace

217

Prayer

—or why we can lose it. But really it is never lost, it only makes itself unknown for a while . . . although I admit it can be a long while."

"Why can't I pray?" "But you do pray. Talking to me like this is a way of praying. I'm sure you know that in the confessional the priest is only an agent, so that you are really talking to God through me. I only hope that I do not block the channel. Besides, this whole subject of prayer is one of the most misunderstood aspects of religion. What is prayer for? Do you know? We send off our petitions for this or that and want replies to come back, instantly, or at least in one or two hours.

"Oh, we know there will not be an actual voice or a flash in the sky, but a response of some sort, that we *do* expect. It is as if we're sending *pneus*. I sometimes think prayerfulness, or even the wish to pray, is better than praying itself, which is so easy for many people, too easy. They get so earnest or tearful and then they *gab* (he used that word) with God."

"What about my sexual troubles, those sins of lust I just confessed? You haven't said anything about them and you haven't given me a penance." "What is there for me to say? I do not think they are such terrible sins. You will not be sent to Hell for them, no, not for them. And what would be the point of my giving you a penance? You are sorry for what you do, isn't that true? Well, do you know I think that to feel contrition for such 'sins' as those is to feel it for all of us as creatures, for our common weaknesses, which we can't help having."

"You sound heretical," I told him, "on this point especially." "Yes," he said after a brief pause, "I suppose I do. But one cannot help touching on heresy at many points if one is to hold on to the Faith."

It was in this that I chiefly detected the strain of weariness

I mentioned before. But I don't want to make too much of this; I don't want to romanticize the priest any more than I may already have done. I love him in my memory, but perhaps my memory has played a trick, transfiguring him along with his words to me. Maybe I've "edited" those words to a higher eloquence or wisdom; we tend to do that? ith those in whom crucial experiences of ours have been lodged.

At the end I asked him how I could go on practicing the Faith in my present state of only partial and increasingly re- luctant belief, adding that I foresaw a time when a sense of insincerity would keep me from doing it altogether. "And what if you do not *practice* it?" he asked me. "What if you do not go to Confession and Communion and all the rest? Do you think you will not still be a Catholic, do you think God will throw you away?"

At this point I told him the story of Rimbaud feeling the "victim" of his own baptism; he hadn't known about it and his reply was "yes, of course." After another pause he said to me, "Look, my dear friend (I'm almost sure he said those three words in French), do what you have to or what you can. I will pray for you. Go in peace."

I went, if not in complete peace then with a greater calm than I had felt for a long time. When I left the church to go back to the hotel the rain had stopped and evening had fallen. I went into a café and had a Pernod. Standing at the bar I thought of how dearly I loved some things about France and Europe: the greater sense and presence of history than we had, the deeper humanity (oh, I knew how subject to sentimentality and literary exoticism this was!), above all the wider acceptance of our human limitations—the very thing, of course, that made Europeans, in our eyes, inferior to ourselves, with our optimism and pragmatic sinew.

Then I left the bar and continued on my way, at some

point finding myself in tears. They weren't from desolation or self-pity, but from . . . what? Relief? Some kind of hope? I have tears in my eyes as I write these lines now.

As I read over what I've written about the incident I fear I may have fashioned it into something "literary," so that it will sound invented, a set piece out of a novel rather like one of Bernanos's or Mauriac's or Greene's. And indeed in my memory the encounter has the quality of such imagined truth: a man, a tormented Catholic, is walking in the rain alongside a cold dark famous river in a foreign country, then goes arbitrarily into a church he comes upon and there meets with an unprecedentedly sympathetic young priest (I guessed him to be in his early thirties, my own age) who speaks his language, understands his spiritual turmoil and has the right words for it all. (My use of quotation marks in having set down our conversation mustn't be taken as an exact transcription from memory. I can't make such a claim. I remember only the gist of the thing, together with some scattered words and phrases and a few whole sentences; but my "inventions" are true to what was said.)

Well, that was how it was, another of those unaccountable circumstances, whose origin I continue to think of as having been *up there*, in which I found myself at times during those years when I needed help beyond the ordinary. It would prove to be the last.

The priest hadn't told me anything about himself except that he had studied English in London during a two-year stay when he was in his late teens and thinking about going into the seminary. I didn't know what order he belonged to, if any; I didn't learn his name.

For some time after I got home to New York I tried even harder to obey the commandments; I went to Mass and Confession more often, steeling myself against the expected scoldings and irrelevant penances; I tamped down my ambition and pride; I "worked" on my erotic propensities, attempting to turn the energy in them toward more acceptable ends, in short to sublimate them. (How touched I am now by my naïveté.)

But I did all this with less desperation than before; I had a diminished terror that if I couldn't bring it off, if I were to "fail" in the Faith, everything wouldn't be lost. The gift that strange young priest had given me was chiefly a renewed sense of mystery and the accompanying increase in hope such a thing can bring. He had indicated to me an unfathomable love beyond the Law, gently showed me that I had an even more subtle and ferocious pride than I had thought—for who was I to make so much of my wrestling match with belief, as though Heaven itself were hanging on the outcome?—and offered me a compassion which for all the formal discrepancies and contradictions I couldn't help thinking of as, yes, Christlike.

I lived on that for a time and then, everything happening at different speeds and taking me continuously by surprise, my life began to change in many significant ways. I lost my battle against ambition, or maybe it would be truer to say that my "humility" began to fall away and so made a space for ambitiousness. Why should I have thought it illicit to want to be successful in the world? All I can say is that I came into the Church in a spirit of self-effacement, saw worldly advancement as inimical to that and so had struggled against my natural desires until under the pressure of external circumstances they broke through.

A central event was the birth in April 1958 of my son, Nicholas. My wife and I had been living with somewhat reduced tension and as we had gotten older we'd decided that whether or not we were fully skilled and resilient enough for being parents we would have a child and take our chances. So we abandoned birth control (resuming it later on) and Nicholas was born. The baby was a source of great satisfaction to both of us, but his presence added to my sense of urgency about my retarded career.

That spring I wrote to the psychoanalyst Theodor Reik at his publishers, asking if he would see me, for I had read his book *Masochism in Modern Man* and had learned from somewhere that he specialized, if I can describe it that way, in writers who were "blocked." Was I such a writer? Not technically, for I had written a great deal for *Jubilee* and a number of other pieces for even more obscure Catholic magazines. But insofar as I hadn't yet written for a nonsectarian world, one where I thought the highest intellectual standards obtained, I indeed felt dammed up.

The analysis I undertook (or "underwent"?) with Reik went on for two or three years and was a fiasco in most respects. For one thing it was interrupted for several months by a heart attack he suffered. For another he was very old and would fall asleep during many of our sessions, thus giving reality to the rueful old joke. So nothing much in me was "analyzed" while I was with him, yet one thing he quite soon gave me, or which I plucked from him, was the courage to make a move toward establishing a broader career.

And so one afternoon late in that spring I went to see James Finn, who at the time was the literary editor of *Commonweal*, which, as I wrote earlier, was a magazine I greatly respected and for which I had been wanting to write for some time.

Commonweal was and is a magazine roughly similar in appearance, format and range of interests to *The New Republic* and *The Nation* (both of which I would later work for), except, naturally, for its Catholic and general religious concerns. What made it so exciting for me to write for it at this time, to the point where I felt I'd begun to "arrive," was that it had a prestige much beyond the closed and basically provincial world of Catholic journalism.

While it was in no sense a "dissenting" or heretical journal, edited as it was by laymen who would not have thought of questioning the Church's authority in purely spiritual or doctrinal matters, it dared to criticize the hierarchy and the Vatican in social and political areas. *Jubilee* had done that too, but much more indirectly, mainly by implication, so that I felt as a liberation *Commonweal's* far greater forthrightness as a magazine of opinion. Even more, its much deeper and bolder cultural coverage excited me with a prospect of real intellectual action.

Jubilee had been at the far edge of what I might call the "machinery" of culture: we were given no theater tickets for a reviewer, were invited to no film screenings; the books we were sent for review were almost all religious in nature. But *Commonweal* was right there, recognized, taken into account.

I think I'm safe in saying that the magazine never had a religious test for its contributors. If a majority of them were Catholic this was due to a communality of shared interests and values, but as far as I knew no one whose mind the editors admired was ever excluded because he or she belonged to a different religion or had no faith at all.

One effect of this, and of the general spirit of open inquiry that obtained there, was a remarkably greater catholicity than is ordinarily found among sectarian or religiously oriented publications; another related one was a sense of freedom from having to toe the line, having to be *religious* in everything you thought and wrote. The spirit showed itself without having to be hooked onto the letter. I remember that at the magazine nobody ever talked much about religion, or at least I didn't talk about it with Finn, Dick Horchler, Dan

Callahan, or Jim O'Gara, the main editors when I was there; we talked about politics (including Church politics), sports, books and the like. (Edward Skillen, the longtime editor in chief, was an extremely quiet, shy man to whom I scarcely spoke at all.)

In all the time I was with *Commonweal* as critic-at-large, literary editor and drama critic, I never wrote anything directly "Catholic" or even religious, nor did I feel any pressure to make my ideas and judgments explicitly accord with some Catholic point of view. That my fundamental moral vision and beliefs did accord with the Church's teaching went without saying, but that had never been where the trouble was. It was on a closer plane of immediate ethics, how to behave in the moment, so to speak, how to deal with the rigidity of the Laws, that I'd begun to feel constraint, but I didn't feel any at *Commonweal.* I didn't have to "fit in," to sacrifice aesthetic truth for moral, say, or pervert my sense of experience in order to bring it into line with announced doctrine. Once at *Jubilee* I gave a favorable review to the Fellini film *La Strada* and received a number of letters protesting my praise for a "sexually immoral" movie; that could never have happened at *Commonweal,* with its far more sophisticated readers.

I had met Jim Finn at some party and figured that he had read pieces of mine in *Jubilee,* so I presumed on that to ask if I could do some reviews for him. When he hesitated, telling me that he was already well stocked with reviews and reviewers and asking me to come back after the summer, something rose up in me, a long-suppressed impulse of self-assertion, so that I burst out: "But I can write better than most of those people you have!" It was a rash thing to say and might have had unfortunate consequences, but as Finn told me later, after we'd become friends, he saw something in my aggressiveness that made him think I was worth taking a chance on.

He gave me a book, a French novel about a group of soldiers trapped in a well-supplied underground bunker during and after World War II. (He later told me he hadn't planned to review it.) It wasn't very good, so, since *Commonweal* was quite receptive to general aesthetic and cultural ideas, I let my review play with the genre the book represented. I handed it in a few days later, Finn liked it and my association with the magazine, which was to last for nearly six years, was born.

While I kept working for *Jubilee* sporadically over the next year or two, I quite soon became a leading reviewer for *Commonweal.* I wrote on all sorts of books—fiction, works of criticism, general culture and so on—and at a later time branched out to do such pieces as an obituary for William Faulkner and a report from Havana, where I had been sent by the magazine as one of a group of journalists invited to Cuba at a time—early 1961—when the Castro regime was strenuously trying to win American goodwill. (I met a number of important people, including the archbishop of Havana, who in a whispery voice assured me that there was full religious freedom under Castro, something I had no way of checking, and, my own goodwill under siege from the scenes of regimentation and strident millennialism before my eyes, from my modest vantage point gave the revolution a mixed notice.)

I had been contributing to *Commonweal* for something over two years when Jim Finn called me at home one day and asked me to have a drink with him later that afternoon. We met at a bar near the office. After some small talk he suddenly asked me if I would like to be the magazine's drama critic. The proposal came as a great surprise to me, for, as I told him, I had no background at all in theater and drama and no greater knowledge of them than any educated person might be expected to have. "I know that," he replied, "but we like your mind and your writing and I'm sure you'll learn the things you have to."

I did learn them. The job wasn't to start until the fall and in the six months between that evening and my first review (of a production of *The Pirates of Penzance*, as it happened) I went to the theater five, six and seven times a week (Off Broadway was beginning to burgeon at the time), read more than five hundred plays and dozens of books on the theater and ended, after that astonishing, demented orgy of self-instruction, feeling that I'd at least got myself ready.

As I look back on it now I can see that something more was at work than this relatively narrow preparation for doing a job. I was moving back to an intellectual realm, or rather I was getting ready fully to occupy one for the first time as more than a marginal figure, or a free-lancer, with what that implies of intermittence and insubstantiality. The irony wasn't lost on me that it had been a Catholic magazine that had propelled me back to the aesthetic life from the spiritual one in Kierkegaard's sense; the truths of dramatic art preoccupied me more now than spiritual ones.

Something I hadn't told Jim that evening in the bar was that I had stopped being a practicing Catholic, though my basic belief remained. This mattered, I thought, because unlike some of the contributors, the magazine's editors were, as far as I knew, all active Catholics, so that I remember thinking that I was withholding information that might have made them think twice about my new roles (during the summer I was asked to become the magazine's literary editor, too, to replace Jim Finn, who was leaving), and surely that's why I didn't say anything.

Still, in my own defense, I knew that I would never do or

write anything that would injure *Commonweal*'s integrity, assuming that I could have gotten away with such sabotage if, for some perverse reason, I'd wanted to. But I hadn't become anti-Catholic, not even in the most hidden or subtle ways; my sympathies were with the magazine's stances, I believed in its usefulness and my affection for it never diminished. And so for my entire two and a half years as an editor of *Commonweal* I was "outside" the Church, and if my colleagues didn't know about it I ask their forgiveness now for having deceived them.

When I try to remember the events that led up to my leaving the Church, becoming a "lapsed" Catholic, I discover that there weren't very many. There isn't much of a "story" here. There were no more crises, no real series of steps I took to disengage myself, few decisions I came to.

The whole leave-taking—which is too precise, as well as too polite; the slipping away—took place in a mist, or at any rate there's a mist over the period now. The months leading up to my baptism remain sharp in my memory, right down to some transient sensual details—of smells, sights and even textures (the tissue-thin paper of the pages in my missal). But my going out of the Church has no such clarity, no thickness of remembered occasion or object. Particular beliefs became obscure, grew faint and at last vanished; urgencies melted and crumbled; attachments loosened and came undone. The world I had been inhabiting shifted and rearranged itself along a new axis.

For it wasn't that I found any new or strengthened reasons for not being able to remain an active Catholic. I didn't, for example, stop believing in God, and God pretty much as the Church had presented Him to me, not merely as the Creator; but I stopped trying to *listen*. I didn't enter into any fiercer warfare with my sexual nature (if anything I was calmer about that, no doubt because I had given up part of the struggle) or conceive new or renewed dislike of my confessors. No, after a while, after my last great effort on my return from Paris (the Battle of the Bulge? a desperate rear-guard action?), it all started to seem irrelevant and, what was worse, although at the time it made my withdrawal easier, I found myself not being able to remember the time when being Catholic had been everything that mattered.

Not that there weren't pain and alarm at what was happening. I remember feeling stabs of fear as the ties began to loosen, a strand here, another there, and I recall the beginning presence in me of a sense of betrayal, on my part, of my doing. The fear, I suppose, was of the unknown, just as it had been before my baptism, and the thought of betrayal rose I'm sure from my having turned down that gift. And so it must have been the need to suppress this, to cover it all over, that lay behind the vagueness and cloudy melancholy with which I took my mind through the process when it was happening and which afflict me now when I try to summon back the time.

So my faith dissolved, went off into thin air, with little turmoil and no dramatic events, except for one, at the very end. It was sometime in the winter of 1959, as best as I can remember. I hadn't been to church, to Mass or Confession for five or six weeks. Then one day I woke up with an unaccountable desire to go, to at least step inside a church, and so late that afternoon I left our new apartment on Eighty-eighth off Madison to go over to St. Ignatius.

It was raining lightly and as I walked the few blocks to the church I pulled my raincoat collar up. I had no umbrella or hat. I've never worn a hat, and that I tell the reader this trivial fact now may be the mark of one last effort to establish my reality.

I'd gone about halfway when without warning I began to

Mystery

have, or be courted by, memories. One after another (as a drowning man is supposed to see his life flash compendiously by) I brought to mind the scene of my baptism in that cavernous church in Colorado Springs, the cop whom I had wanted to tell about God having captured me, the monks chanting at the monastery in Vermont, Ruth, Father Walsh (whose library was right next to the church steps), the voice of the priest in the confessional in Paris, even the apparitional nuns of my childhood. As I turned the corner of Eighty-fifth and Park I was crying, softly. (So many occasions for tears in this book, and such different origins for them all!)

It was early evening, gloomy and chilly, as I started to climb the stairs to the main entrance. There were seven or eight steps, as I recall, and when I reached the fourth or fifth I stopped. I tried to go on but I couldn't move; standing there, trembling, I thought of the occasion in the public library when I had tried to leave but had been impelled back to the Gilson book. (But how different this was! In the library an invisible force had been *up to something* and I had been in its field; here there was only powerlessness, my own unconscious resistance.)

Once again putting on a clown show or mime act for any onlooker—the street was in fact deserted—I scraped my feet, trying to lift them, at one point with my hands pulling on my thighs. I looked up at the church doors and stood there in the soft rain, paralyzed.

After a while, maybe twenty or thirty seconds, I gave up, turned around, went down the steps and headed for home. As I walked, at first with a faint buzzing in my head and a tightness in my throat, a memory came to me of the incident of the uneven paving stones near the end of *Remembrance of Things Past*. This is the moment when the narrator feels the past unlocking itself, as memory becomes triumphant

229

and time returns to its sources; such a glorious victory for the imagination, I've always thought. But under my feet there had been something very nearly the opposite of Proust's triumph. For me time was coming to an end and not returning, liberated, to a beginning.

What did I replace my Catholicism with, if anything? Or a better way to put it might be: what became true in me afterward, in those internal spheres we variously refer to as soul, psyche, spirit? I had forgotten it for years but now I remember that I tried for a time to go back to Judaism. But I'd never really been there, so the effort was fated quickly to expire. I remember one strange thing I did at this time. I sent a letter to the cathedral of Colorado Springs demanding that they strike my name from their baptismal records, as though by this action I could expiate some residual guilt. They didn't reply, for which I soon became grateful.

As I write about my spiritual condition after I left the Church I have an impulse to look up some notes I took from a book by Philippe Ariès called *The Hour of Our Death*, which I reviewed a few years ago.

The Hour of Our Death. From the Hail Mary: "Pray for us sinners now and at the hour . . ."

I find this passage: "There are two ways of not thinking about death: the way of our technological civilization which denies death and refuses to talk about it; and the way of traditional civilizations, which is not a denial but a recognition of the impossibility of thinking about it directly or for very long."

I've copied this out because the chief change in me of attitude or morale after my faith left was that I stopped thinking about death, or rather I only thought about it when it somehow managed to get my attention, as a matter of palpable threat, a question, then, on the one hand of hygiene to ward it off and on the other of potential insult. Which is to say that I didn't really think about it; I denied it by refusing any longer to consider it as *within* my life, with all the consequences of that for my spirit, my soul. And so I became largely secular, which in this context means I came to dwell almost wholly in the immediate.

More than twenty-five years have gone by since that evening on the church steps, and this is a little less than two-thirds of my adult life. The words are easy to set down, these abstractions denoting units of chronology, just as the mathematical calculation behind them is also abstract and simple to do; but I feel a cold wind blowing over those facts. I make another little calculation and the wind gusts up again: I have been out of the Church five times as long as I was in it.

(Steady! No more tears. Statistics shouldn't have that power. Be witty at this point, or at least pleasant. Anything but more tears.)

"Out of the Church" is a peculiar expression, much more resembling "out of sorts" or "out of luck" than, say, "out of the country." For what is it you're out of? During these twenty-five years I've physically been inside various Catholic churches on a number of occasions, for funerals or memorial services for friends, a few baptisms of children, once or twice for weddings. But I haven't been there as a member of the flock, and though I've always had trouble with that expression, suggesting as it does all those sheep trundling along, bumping into one another with their thick heads swaying and collies nipping at their heels, the metaphor tells against the far thinner sense of belonging—to anything—I now have. I was *inside* once, now I'm elsewhere.

No going to Confession or taking Communion, no Easter duties to fulfill, no joy (or, I must be true to it, mostly theoretical joy) at Christmas or sorrow on Good Friday. My missal sits on one of the highest shelves of my library, among a dwindling number of Catholic books: five or six works on Saint Joan, which I'll always hang on to: the *Imitation of Christ;* Unamuno's *Tragic Sense of Life* and *Agony of Christianity;* Romano Guardini's *The Lord;* some philosophical or theological works by Catholic "existentialists" like Gilson, Jacques Maritain, Max Picard, Emmanuel Mounier, Gabriel Marcel, and so on. Every so often I'll take one down and leaf through it and it will strike me as an outdated travel book, an aging Baedeker to a country I once visited. (But the Bernanos, Mauriac and Greene novels go on existing near at hand among my shelves of fiction.)

Such remoteness now, such a distance from what it once was. But as I think back I remember how some practices and habits died hard. For a long time I found myself uneasy at the thought of eating meat on Fridays, until at last that remnant of sacrifice and obedience was gone. Again, for years I would react to a piece of bad news or a sudden fear by crossing myself, and to the death of someone I knew or the report of some disaster—a bus falling off a cliff in Mexico, a ferry capsizing in India—by saying a quick Our Father. And until quite recently I would ritually say a Hail Mary under my breath before starting out to drive on a highway, especially if my children were with me, or when the plane I was in was taking off or landing.

I've often thought about these things. Was it residual superstition? Staying on the safe side? Hanging on to formulas for the deflection of evil? All I know is that during my time as a Catholic my nerves and muscles and all the pathways of my unconscious mind had been so imbued with those practices that they became second nature and stayed on as tag ends of the sacred when my life went back to being "profane."

Sacred and profane. What a gulf, what antipathy there is between those words! Yet all that "profane" originally meant in its Latin root was "outside the temple," and later, still neutrally, in medieval Latin and French, "not pertaining to what is sacred or biblical . . . civil as distinguished from ecclesiastical." At what point did "profanity" come into use as a synonym for bad language, cursing, with its implications at first of hostility to the sacred order and after that, in our own spiritually diluted age, of a defiance of propriety? My life after I went "outside the temple" hasn't been profane in either of those senses. It's been what it has been, set *against* nothing and taking its course on such grounds without structures to house the sacred as I've been able, or been compelled, to rest upon.

Strictly speaking this memoir is finished now, the tale of my coming to, being in and leaving the Catholic Church. Yet I feel an incompleteness, an obligation to bring things up to the present, since if my story has interested the reader I imagine that he or she will want to know something about its aftermath. And so, as briefly as I can, I'll set down the main events and facts of the twenty-five years since I stopped practicing as a Catholic, and after that, in order to fulfill the expectations that books of this kind arouse, offer some reflections on what the experience meant to me and some thoughts on whether or not I've learned, as I mentioned at the beginning, why I wanted to write the book.

I was *Commonweal*'s drama critic and literary editor for over two and a half years. During this period I also began to write for many other publications: *Theater Arts, The New York Times Book Review, The New Republic, Commentary*, and so on. Then in the spring of 1964 I was asked to become the drama critic of *Newsweek*. I had been averaging about seventy-five dollars a week at *Commonweal*, and since

Newsweek offered me three hundred dollars to start and because I was on my own now, having separated definitively from my wife, I overcame my apprehensions about writing for a "mass" magazine and took the job.

While I was at *Newsweek*, where I had much freedom within the limits of the situation, I went on writing for other publications, on fiction and ideas as well as drama. Then during the academic year of 1964–65 I did my first teaching, having been asked to fill in for Eric Bentley, who had for years taught a big modern drama class at Columbia and who had been a powerful influence on my own thinking about the theater. I was exceedingly nervous before my first lecture—all those smart-alecky undergraduates!—but I quickly got into it and soon found that I enjoyed teaching and was rather good at it.

I've often thought that I had certain advantages in coming to teaching as late as I did. I didn't have to climb the professional ladder or participate in academic politics; I'd already published so I was in no danger for not doing so; I hadn't had time to become infected with any of the occupational diseases of the academy—rote methods, hazy or pompous pedagogical theories, intellectual conservatism; most liberating of all, I didn't have to protect a bit of territory by minute and ferocious specialization. In an important sense I was and remain an amateur.

Just before I went to *Newsweek* I joined the Open Theater and was with the group for nearly two years, as what was called an "adviser" but is better described as an intellectual presence, my colleague in this work of aesthetic and philosophical investigation being my close friend Gordon Rogoff.

It was an exhilarating time for the hastening movement of alternative or "serious" theater in New York. At the Open Theater we worked with almost no money, moving by our wits; on fire with ideality and enthusiasm, we were sustained by intense camaraderie and our energy as exponents of new visions of what theater might be. We fell on our faces at times but some of what we did was inspiring to ourselves and others. Naturally, we couldn't have foreseen it, but in the years to come the Open Theater would take on an almost legendary status, one that's become enriched with nostalgia since the group's formal dissolution more than twelve years ago.

After I'd been there awhile I was asked to direct plays, which I'd never done before, and so satisfying, so heady in its pleasures was this work that I came close at one point to throwing everything else up in order to make directing my career. This alarmed me because I saw myself having to give up writing and I couldn't do that; I *was* a writer, of however peripheral a kind, whereas directing, no matter how successful I might become at it, would always be a role, a series of actions making up a place in the world, and not a self. The distinction isn't very clear, I know, but I felt it keenly at the time. So I fought off the temptation and indeed left the group because I was afraid I might someday yield to it.

In the fall of 1967 I resigned from *Newsweek* and accepted an invitation to teach at the Yale School of Drama; I've been there ever since, except for one year when I was a visiting professor at City College in New York. I'd grown tired of the hoopla and banality of Broadway and of having to "cover" all the big openings (though I was free to write about some smaller, more truthful occasions too, which is what sustained me). I remember once saying to a friend that like the happy families in the opening sentence of *Anna Karenina*, which are happy in the same way, all bad Broadway musicals and melodramas are bad in the same manner. So I went off to Yale, where I've had much satisfaction and pleasure, and with the exception of a recent two-year stint as drama critic for *The Nation* I've not gone back to being an observer of the theater on a regular basis.

To run through everything else now. From 1968 to 1970 I served as the literary editor of *The New Republic*, doing the job from my New York apartment and commuting, as I always have, to Yale. In the early seventies I was on the editorial board of *Performance*, a fine theater magazine that unfortunately lasted only a year or two, and throughout the decade I was a contributing editor of *Partisan Review*. I published my first book, *The Confusion of Realms*, in 1969 and have published three more since then. I've had my share of fellowships and grants—a Guggenheim, Rockefeller and Ford travel grants (such great fortunes behind our work at the margins!)—and of prizes: the George Jean Nathan Award for drama criticism, the Morton Dauwen Zabel Award of the American Academy and Institute of Arts and Letters, for criticism. I have an honorary degree from Grinnel College. From 1981 to 1983 I was president of the American center of PEN, the international writers' association, an honor of which I'm most proud and a task which I hope I met with fidelity.

I married again in 1966 and had times of much happiness as well as of stress and sorrow during the fourteen years the marriage lasted; when it ended, against my desire, I mourned and was thrown into despair for a while. An unparalleled joy was the birth of my daughters, to whom this book is dedicated: Priscilla on May 1, 1970, and Claire on July 14, 1971. (Wonderful birth dates! Twice we were in France on Bastille Day for Claire to pretend to think that all the ceremony and celebration were for her, and I've dreamed of taking Priscilla to Moscow for May Day.) Like that of my son Nicholas, their half brother whom they dearly love—"doesn't feel like half a brother to me," one of them said when she was about five—their childhoods were a renewal and replenishment for me; now their adolescent lives are continuing sources of revelation and disconcerting love.

And so I have lived, multiplied and, as they say, made something of myself, and am far from being happy. (The *pursuit* of happiness is all we're entitled to, boy!) My erotic self is somewhat calmer these days, but the old doppelgänger, that admirer and fantasist of female prowess and dominion, still trails me, sometimes at a manageable distance and sometimes right up my back.

There are moments when I like living alone but more when I yearn for the presence of a mate and when, most often on days when my daughters stay over and I'm inserted temporarily and, yes, it's not too strong a word, achingly into their lives again, I long for the fullness of a family, its continuity and volatile, encompassing reality, all blessings and oppressions.

Along with that I suffer from the absence of intimacy with my son. It's not exactly an estrangement, and it's slowly being healed, but some sort of psychic distance crept in between us when he was in his adolescence, which he went through in part away from me, in another state. The delinquencies were surely mine; perhaps, chiefly, that I kept from sharing with him the large outline at least of my emotional life, my "secrets," my particular kind of maleness, which I must have thought was too much for him to understand. I believe he'll understand it now.

And I believe, too, that my two wives, Esther and Lynn, as well as several other women I've loved, but not well enough, will understand better what I was and forgive me for it. . . .

I shall probably live long. My father died a few years ago at ninety-one (he stopped smoking when he was sixty-five;

I'll do it at that age too), my mother died recently at something over ninety-five. I have good genes; biology, nature, has been kind to me. I'm told I look much younger than my age. I have plans for several more books, one of them an inquiry into and celebration of Saint Joan. I have friends, a place in the world, an identity.

But I'm not happy, I've less happiness than I once had, I haven't been pursuing it in the right way. And the thought has come to me more than once of late that I may have lost my chance on that evening twenty-five years ago when my feet wouldn't move on the church steps. Once again, despite my injunctions, tears start up in my eyes. I think of this book's epigraph from Bernanos's *Diary of a Country Priest*. To write truthfully about yourself requires that you be hard, almost pitiless, yet such severity immediately brings about its counter-statement: self-pity.

I sit in a cab on my way to the airport. The entire space around me—the plastic and metal perforated partition that protects the driver from the gun or knife I might have, the back door and sides, even the roof—is covered with stickers that exhort or proclaim: READ YOUR BIBLE! PRAY EVERY DAY! CHRIST DIED FOR OUR SINS! GOD ISN'T DEAD, I SPOKE TO HIM THIS MORNING! The signs are particularly ugly: their colors, which are mostly strident reds and smudgy blacks, their blocky lettering, the exclamation points. But what's most obnoxious about them is that they've been mass-produced in some factory where in different rooms, most likely, other stickers are being turned out for greasy spoons to declare that WE MAKE THE BEST CUP OF COFFEE IN THE WORLD or command us to HAVE A NICE DAY.

Everything about this display of aggressive, derivative religiosity offends and repels me. Once again I'm embarrassed by the idiot vulgarity in which so much religion is bathed in

Loss of Mystery

our time and I have a sudden impulse of protectiveness toward God, wanting to get Him out of the hands of self-righteous zealots like this stupid cabbie (whose face I can't see).

Immediately I'm invaded by doubt, self-accusation and, at the end of it, remorse. Who and what am I to take so lofty a stance, what rights have I in the matter? Do I think I can speak for "true" religion when I've no more connection to it than I had when I was an atheist? I might as well be an atheist but I'm not; this has been brought home to me by the surprising desire I've just had, the wish, egotistical perhaps but also, I think, oddly honorable, to succor God.

In the plane (to London for a PEN meeting, I think) I go over the arguments in my favor. Flannery O'Connor's remark about a certain type of fundamentalist comes back to me: "They call themselves holy but holiness costs and so far as I can see they don't pay anything."

Before I bring myself to ask what *I've* been paying, I run through the indictment I've drawn up of that movement within Protestantism that's provided much of the basis for Sunday-supplement articles about "America's Religious Revival." I start with the narrowness and xenophobia and go on to the materialism, the greed to have it all ways. But those things are boringly obvious. What I detest most is their specifically religious rhetoric, their pulpit oratory.

The ground of my abhorrence isn't that they flout reason, although some of them, like the Creationists, do it in a particularly oafish way. I'm not worried about reason, which has more than enough defenders and anyway can take care of itself. No, it's precisely the mystical I want to protect, or rather mystery; purely rational minds, monsters of practicality and steely logic, attack from one side while the sects come marching from the opposite direction, so that between them mystery is ruined.

Mystery

239

They make divinity so available, these people who speak of God as their "best friend." They make Him so much like themselves. Christ is a golf buddy, a business partner, someone with capital and a halo. ("Wealth is God's way of rewarding those who put Him first . . . put Jesus first in your stewardship and allow Him to bless you financially."—Jerry Falwell.)

They turn God into a citizen, a jingoist at that. He's a consumer, a go-getter, a success story. They give Him their own attributes and desires, but if religion means anything it means the awareness of otherness, radical difference from ourselves and, on the moral side, perfection such as we, unfit for the job, can only attempt with enormous inadequacy to inch toward. We can't *use* God, He's not a technique. We can't even conceive of Him, as the Father anyway, except by a hugely difficult abstract process of analogy. Yet they talk about Him as if He were a football coach or the *head of a department.*

Why don't they suffer? Why doesn't it cost them anything, as Flannery said? God, I want to hear sad tales, stories of pain and incapacity, of betrayal and despair, stories of *what we're like.* Or at least I want real words, not this rhetoric of inane piety. Why does every born-again person, every evangelical preacher, sound the same? Is God such a bad playwright?

I stop here, still worked up but beginning to feel contrition. In truth, I force myself to see, the vulgarity, the degradation of God into an agency of material usefulness, a public utility, is something to be pitied. Isn't it one result of American pragmatism, by which I don't mean formal, philosophical pragmatism such as John Dewey's but the ways of utility we've been instructed in by so many of our myths as a people? Doesn't it come in part from our bias against the transcendent, history, the invisible and all values that rest on a principle of deferral? In any case, how can you condemn people who see by their lights and who at least have stepped outside the circle of sterility, the solipsism in which we're all fastened, even if they end by dragging otherness back in?

And where are *you* now? I sit at the typewriter and my mind turns to the priest in Paris telling me that God wouldn't toss me away, that I'd still be a Catholic even after I stopped physically (and mentally too?) conducting myself like one. I very much want to believe him and I'm surprised that I do. Against all my expectations writing this book has reawakened desire in me, if not for going formally back into the Church then at least for not being entirely separated from it. Still, I don't see how I can interpret that French priest's assurances in my favor.

(Try. Make an inventory. List the ways, even the most marginal ones, in which you're still connected to Catholicism, still religious. Be subtle, but not overly so; take account of residual yearnings, no matter how inchoate, and of those occasional stabs of regret, but don't credit yourself with "goodwill" unless you can prove it.)

I believe in God, that's to begin with. I'll never be an atheist again, the dagger of baptism changed all that forever. And I'm certainly not an agnostic, which has always struck me as a waffling, ignoble cast of mind; a person either believes that God exists or he or she doesn't. To be "open" to the possibility flatters with the liberality of it all and costs nothing. And it's God I believe in, not "a" God or "the" Gods. There are no Gods. Monotheism wasn't an invention but a discovery. There's only Him.

But what kind of belief do I have, what's the good of it? I don't pray and I don't act sacrificially and I never think about Him except when He comes up in conversation as more than an expletive, which can still happen, if rarely, or

Mystery

_____RICHARD GILMAN

when I'm working on this book. And even then He's mainly just a figure in my narrative, an *occasion* for my thought.

Yes (the other, dueling voice says), but notice how you go on using the uppercase *H*. It's more than a mere reflex or obedience to common usage. You believe He's still there, behind the twenty-five years of silence, and you don't want to be disrespectful. No, that's weak. When the pronoun presents itself in the movement of your sentences you press the shift key out of a desire to please and honor Him in the only way you can, trivial as it may seem.

It's trivial. Think of something else. Well, you're always coming to the defense of Catholicism (and of what you think of as "sincere" religion in general) whenever you hear it attacked, at a literary dinner party, say, or at one of those mad symposia on post-Freudian or post-Christian or post-whatever Man. You remember having read somewhere that "anti-Catholicism is the anti-Semitism of the liberal," and though this was more true a generation ago you see it displayed often enough for you to speak up and call people on it, more apologetically than fiercely, I must admit.

Go on.

There are those pangs of regret, widely spaced to be sure.

And?

Well . . .

So that's it. That's the lot.

No, one more thing, your respect for mystery.

Would you say a little about that?

Sure. You think of mystery as what remains, savingly, after we've explained or used reason on everything we can and are nevertheless left with dissatisfaction and, worse, oppression, sadness, loss and dismay. You once looked to art for salvation of this sort, for relief from facts, the tyranny of the way things are, your own finiteness, and you still look there, if with diminished ardor and expectations. And then,

242

without canceling out art, you became religious and were
stricken and exhilarated by being brought face-to-face with
mystery of the most fundamental sort.

But that was *then*.

I know, you've changed. But it seems to me that your disgruntlement and some particulars of the critique you're continually making of the present world have to do with the
absence of mystery, of that other dimension where, as you
wrote earlier, there are two kinds of time and material things
are given a buoyancy because they matter less. I think that's
religious.

Someone asked me recently what my "position" was in
regard to religious belief these days and I told him that I was
a lapsed Jewish-atheist-Catholic. Fallen from all three, a tri-
ple deserter! There's wryness and melancholy in this as well
as a contradiction. Well, I meant the part about atheism as a
joke, of course, yet not quite only as one.

We commonly use the word "lapsed" to denote something
running out and not being renewed, like a period of time, a
membership or a subscription. I'd been an atheist once,
which, in my youthful bravado, I regarded as a position, a
point of view that suggested membership in a community:
the fellowship of unbelievers. A bit fanciful, no doubt, especially in today's climate, yet when I gave up atheism as a
committed way of looking at existence and stepped over or
leaped up to religion, I had a slight feeling of having let
something run out, of having dropped a membership.

As for Judaism, we don't ordinarily speak of lapsing from
it, though there'd surely be some pertinence if we did. The
similarity to dropping out of Catholicism is that you no
longer observe the religion you were—in almost every
case—born into, you don't go to synagogue or hold seders or
pray to Yahweh. The difference is that you stay Jewish in

your bones and pores, there's no lapsing from that; changed names or nose bobs won't do it, because being a Jew has very much in common with being Italian or Hungarian, or being black or white.

But a lapsed Catholic: that's a solid term. On some kind of hunch, an anxious one, I look up "lapsed" in my O.E.D. and find a definition that quite shocks me. To be lapsed in the religious sense originally meant to have "foresworn Christianity under the threat of persecution" and thus to have fallen into a "lower" state because of cowardice. After reading this I can't any longer take refuge in the technical, more or less neutral, contemporary sense of the term. I didn't forswear Christianity out of fear, certainly not fear of being thrown to the modern equivalent of lions, yet it may not make any difference; my having lapsed could still mean that I've been judged as *lower* by an invisible tribunal. I shrug off the notion but it only moves a short distance from me and waits.

There is a line from Camus's *The Stranger* that has been much in my thoughts of late. After not having read the novel in more than thirty years I recently read it again for a course in fiction and film I've been giving at Yale. As he awaits his execution Meursault, the man who has killed "because of the sun," says these words about the fatality that has struck him: "From the dark horizon of my future a sort of slow persistent breeze had been blowing towards me, all my life long, from the years that were to come."

The line is very beautiful, even more so in French, and its rhythms of meaning, its image of time reversed, the future (in Meursault's case his coming death) wafting over the present and so in a manner shaping it, affects and troubles me. For I think this: did I fashion my conversion or lend myself to it in such a way that it was bound to end, never having been allowed to take true hold? Had I already in the early days and months of that event, even in its moments of exultation, been planning its overthrow, secretly conspiring with the person I tenaciously wished to be, in defiance of the one I had just, presumably, become?

And under the wind from my future that was preparing an ultimate destination for me was this person I craved to be—or maybe just couldn't abandon—lower and darker than I could acknowledge? It had been painful for me to go into the Church and painful to leave it. Didn't these sufferings come from my having to make bitter relinquishments and rueful choices in each case? To become a Catholic I had to give up much of my past and a dream of self-sufficiency and then turn myself over to the unknown, the dangerous, indeed the alien. To leave the Church I had to repudiate my previous surrender in order to return to a seemingly freer, but unsupported and ungraced, self. What had I truly wanted?

For it was, and always is, a question of will, conscious or not. "Father, thy will and not mine be done": such is the formulary prayer for the situation of egoism vs. divinity. In the writhings of the struggle I told myself that I simply couldn't determine God's will for me, once He had stopped intervening directly in my life, stopped giving those clear persuasive signs, or else that His will had been obscured, even subverted, by His inadequate representatives on earth. But I can't take comfort now from either of these explanations.

A stiff-necked Jew, maybe that's what I've been. I'd heard the phrase, of course, but never imagined it could apply to me. No, the image is still that of an old man with a dirty beard and ungiving eyes, dressed in a robe and sandals, leaning on a stick and hurling curses at the Law. No bowing of the head for this fellow . . . hardness, defiance, all energy gathered into a spear of self-assertion and refusal to yield. Had I been like that? Does "stiff-necked" mean insisting on the letter of the Law, or rather on what *you* think the spirit of it should be, demanding one's rights, which in my case meant above all God's direct and unwavering attention to me? I think I've been like that.

I know I've been a rationalizer, a subtle schemer after a "truth" about my actions that would keep my conscience disarmed. And I know that beneath those rationalizations I fell back into self-commiseration because the battle against carnality and ambition—which had come more and more to look like aspects of the same primary force, alarming, guilt-ridden—had become too much for me. In this retreat I had left God behind. I wasn't to be solicited anymore.

Along with my hunger for eternal life I had moved toward conversion seeking the relief that comes from turning over to a "higher" power some of the burden of selfhood, self*ness*, the swollen aspect of it I've been calling solipsism: the entirely self-referential, self-determining, self-validating. Egotism. But to spring clear of that, to be relieved in the way I sought, means to be prepared to submit, to give over. It also means to be able to trust that your humanity, your "natural" part, won't be warped or obliterated.

As I write, my mind fills with images and thoughts of such warping, most of it sexual, and of the cost of holding out between piety and bodily desire. Spots of deadness seem to appear on some believers, deaths before the real one. I think of the dead woman, the suicide from whose embrace I fled on that evening in my friend's apartment, and of a sad brilliant friend of mine, an Irish-Catholic who has spent much of his life roasting in the flames of alcoholism and homosexuality. His drinking rose from his guilt over his sexual nature and *that*, he knew, was condemned by his ancestral faith.

Some escape these blights, some are made lively and animate by religion. What is their secret? Couples who move gracefully and without strain in their carnality, licit and, apparently, in control; they believe in the body (within limits: passion must be legalized, etc.) and they have children, sometimes many, without loss of ardor. They're square. I don't understand them. What is their secret?

Most of us can't make it this way. The garden of earthly delights, what is it for, why is it there? To school us in the virtue of abnegation? As a means for us to demonstrate to Him, by spurning or chastening the flesh, our recognition of the primacy of the spirit and so of the hierarchy of mortal things? But *is* the spirit higher than the body? Is eternity only inhabited by spirits? But we've been promised the resurrection of the body. Will such bodies have memories of this life of the senses and if not, what was this life for? What a cruel notion that it should only have been a test.

My thoughts trail off . . . I see the body and the spirit mutually fulfilled, but only in the ideal, as a theologian's sketch. But now I remember the time when I did trust that my natural self would be mysteriously redeemed and its yearnings and the things it admired—surely some of them were worthy—but above all its sorrowfulness and joys, its dilemmas, crack-ups and boredoms, its *having been*, would be just as mysteriously preserved. But for all my avowed respect for mystery it seems that I couldn't wait for its operations to take effect, didn't trust that it would happen. And I don't trust it now.

As I read over these last lines something makes me turn back to what I wrote earlier about how my attitude toward death changed after I stopped practicing the Faith. I no longer understood it, however dimly, as being within my life, both a moral and an ontological question and fact—and the great locus of mystery—but saw it as purely material, an impending blow from outside that ought to be staved off as long as possible. I spoke of having become secular, an inhabitant wholly of this world, which regards mystery as an affront. And now a fissure opens up in my thoughts and a chill runs through me on this warm summer day. For I suddenly become aware that there may have been a great deficiency in my reading of my life. *Mortality and Immortality:* that was the title I had in mind when I began this book, and I think I've made mistakes in my understanding of both.

I wanted not to die, I craved eternal life. I thought I was protesting finiteness, having only this body, only so many years. I thought I wanted my felicity to be extended, as one who says: please, I don't want it to end. But my felicity was intermittent, and what I mostly had was a problematic, afflicted, pseudolyrical, aspiring self, a self *manqué*. And seeing this makes me push further, into a true terror and upheaval.

Could it have been that my wish not to die, my *making so much of it*, was in fact a desire not to live, not to live fully? (What a swamp I'm in!) Was I in flight from carnality and its responsibilities (the chief of these is to stay with it, neither disgusted nor blithe; to hear its voice but hear others too). Was my thirst for transcendence a desertion of my creatureliness? And did my craving for eternity resemble the madness of the man or woman who frantically disguises the ravages of age and so goes against the calm, implacable, terrifying, lovely order of things? To mask oneself in this way is to try to forestall death, outwit it; to bellow about eternal life is to try to outshoot it.

We die, living as an aspect of dying, and by this I don't mean the comfortable literary conceit that we head for death from the cradle. Life and death are twins, reciprocities, they depend on each other. But we don't see it. We're taught about nature's grand scheme, how life gives way, yields, is replaced, perpetuated, the triumph of the species. But we don't apply this to ourselves. How can we think of ourselves, *conduct* ourselves, as members of a species, like baboons or fruit flies?

The best some of us have is a thin, secretly disconsolate acceptance that we'll live on in our children or works or in the memories of others. Memories! What good is that if we don't know about it? And that isn't it, anyway. We're not supposed to evade or defeat death by such imagined prolongations of ourselves but to fuse life and death in ourselves in, yes, a carnal embrace.

Sex and death. Eros and Thanatos. I think of Freud, of course, but even more at this moment of a book by Georges Bataille, translated as *Death and Sensuality*, which I read and was shaken by some years ago but some of whose ideas I must have suppressed in my memory because of their danger to my fragile equanimity. Bataille wrote about eroticism as an "invention," a human structure added to biology, and because of its existence as sheer nonutilitarian pleasure, a threat to the world of "work," duty, institutional control, which helps account for so much historical repression of the sexual realm. Then he went on to speak of the relations between the sexual act and death, their mysterious, almost unbearable affinity.

I was familiar with some of this: the "little death" as a description of orgasm, the obliteration of personality and individual being at the moment of climax. But what I didn't know then, the thing I've hidden from myself after I learned it from Bataille (earlier, in cruder form, from Freud), is that we partly wish such obliteration, the escape from the bounded self, from time and responsibility and our lamentable separateness. We wish and fear it and live in that tension, just as we do in the paradox that death is necessary in order for life to be.

I can't go much further with this! (Go further, a little more.) A woman dear to me told me recently that she thought that divinity pulled the soul, the immortal part, out of the self, the way sexual joy did. I knew what she meant, but then I threw against her—a born Catholic, a woman with "sins" of lust in her dossier—the fact of the Church, its formal proscriptions; how, I asked her, could she go on feeling herself Catholic while *disobeying*? I live, she said, I'm a sinner, the Church is for sinners, I won't give it up, it doesn't know everything and it's not synonymous with God. But I belong to it, and so do you, if your hurt and pride could let you see it.

I think now: sex and death have been the dominant words in this book, the rubrics under which I've tried to organize what's happened to me. Sex and death and mystery. I came into the Church because of death and left because of sex. I didn't trust mystery, which is the same thing as saying I didn't give myself.

If you believe in mystery in the religious sense, trusting in its eventual yielding of new redemptive knowledge, then it's death (and sex as both death's denial and its sister) that's at the center of your trust. Death is what we hand over to divinity, everything about it: the fear, the lack of understanding, its insidiousness and blatancy and beauty, its reign. Religion is about death or it's about nothing, which is why, as I think I wrote a long time ago in this book, when death receded, got deferred, religion lost its urgency and rationale—a weak word for the violent truth of something beyond our powers but within our longing.

Always the question of mystery. I see now that I continue to believe in God, impotently, grudgingly, in the face of His silence, because of the miracles, those visitations that prompted me and seduced me into faith. And this is the ground of my present unease, no, my anguish. Why was I visited? Why were so much wit and creativity (I'm not being blasphemous in this anthropomorphism; I don't want God to be like me, I want Him far more deft of thought) expended on my behalf?

I'm only one among all the others, dear God. So why me? And why did you pull out? You were supposed to teach me how both to live and die, so why did you cancel the lessons?

These aren't fair questions and I know it but feel a sudden burst of rage against you and want to scream in your ear: it's your fault, *I'm* your fault.

No, you offered me Grace, how can I get round it? And I spurned it, how can I get round that?

I have my share of the stock of visible or determinable things. I have my life still, but only one kind of time. Eternity, which I once pursued, is slipping away, and I mourn that, even though I'm tired and have lost the keenness of that time when, though I deceived myself, I wanted my youth to be extended forever. And I don't know where my soul is.

There was once someone to whose judgment I submitted. How do I judge myself now, with what criteria that aren't self-serving, and how do I bear the burden of being both magistrate and accused? I move toward death; I'm not being theatrical, for I do move toward it, and it's in me once again and not simply a metaphor or a blank and inconsequential end to being. And there *is* something to be judged, which the standards of the world can't handle.

* * *

I'm paralyzed, or nearly so. I can't finish this book. For more than two weeks I've waited in front of its last potential lines like someone standing at the edge of the water on a freezing day, shivering and unable to make the plunge. I think again of my death and then of a line in Graham Greene's *The Power and the Glory* which I copied out and now look up in my notes. One should never rely on a deathbed conversion, he wrote, for "penitence was the fruit of long training and discipline."

Yet it isn't quite the power of repentance I'm hoping for, nor, whatever my distress, do I anguish over my possible damnation. I want to be "saved" (who would wish to be lost?) but outside the temple I don't know what that means anymore. I only know that I don't want to die as an act purely of nature, of this world; I want my poor value to exist past me, somewhere else. I want my tears to be wiped away and those of the people I love. I want to make sense of everything, but more than that, to make peace with it.

And I can't finish the book because when I do this history and inquest, which I secretly hoped would settle my "case" once and for all, will come to an end and I'm terrified that I'll have failed to give some vital piece of evidence or, far worse, have deceived myself entirely. Have I been too easy on myself? Too hard?

I won't again have the chance to capture truth of this order, the chance to take it all up, sifting through it, measuring, explaining, trying to justify and not to justify. I had a shot at it, as they say, and I'm frightened I may have muffed it. I set out to tell it the way it happened, but did I?

Against my modern idea that uncertainty is privileged and conclusions are alway premature, I want to have come to a denouement. Will those readers who went through this book with goodwill and openness to me feel disappointed because I gave them nothing definitive, no calls to order, no models for behavior or moral resting place, and left them with the sight of me still pedaling in midair?

I finish the book and take my chances.